"W. Edwards Deming said, 'Every system is perfectly designed to get the results it gets.' The Western church's hierarchical leadership has achieved the results it was designed to—declining attendance, closing seminaries, and a stream of moral failures. Thank God that E. K. Strawser wrote this book to disciple pastors and ministry leaders to reassess the system. *You Were Never Meant to Lead Alone* offers an inspiring and practical blueprint for sustainable, disciple-making churches where all of God's people flourish. This is not a path forward—it's a return to how the church was always meant to operate."

Eric Hoke, founder of I Help Pastors Get Jobs and author of *Market Street Pastor*

"In an age and culture where poor leadership in the church has left liminal space in its wake, E. K. Strawser, seeking the best path forward, provides a clear and viable understanding of shared leadership culture and how to implement it. This is a must-read for church and organizational leaders."

Rowland Smith, national director of Forge America Missional Training Network and author of *Life Out Loud*

"*You Were Never Meant to Lead Alone* is a timely call to reclaim the power of shared leadership. E. K. Strawser challenges the Western church's default to hierarchical, male-dominated, pastor-centric models, offering a vision rooted in Ephesians 4's Apostles, Prophets, Evangelists, Shepherds, and Teachers (APEST) framework— leadership that is dynamic, interdependent, and missionally engaged. This book is both prophetic and practical, equipping leaders to move beyond isolation and exhaustion into a dynamic, communal way of living and leading."

Deb and Alan Hirsch, authors and founders of Forge Missional Training Network, Movement Leaders Collective, and other innovative organizations

"E. K. Strawser's book is very timely for Christian leaders of today as well as future leaders. I personally grew up and was trained under the paradigm of pastoral leadership in singularity rather than a shared reality. Strawser's insights bring to the forefront the need and benefits of shared leadership within the body of Christ. The idea of leaders operating within their multiplicity of spiritual giftedness certainly finds its origins within the biblical text. Ephesians 4 certainly confirms and affirms this reframing presented by Strawser in such a way that will prove to be very beneficial for all leaders."

Wayne D. Faison, executive director of the Baptist General Association of Virginia

"In my work over the last few years, we have recognized that the church is moving from clergy led/lay supported to lay led/clergy supported. Eun Strawser helps us utilize the Ephesians 4 framework to delineate and embrace shared leadership based on maturity and not popularity or charisma, until we have unity in the faith and knowledge of Jesus and all come to maturity (Eph. 4:13). Thanks, Eun, for the reminder and the challenge!"

Dee Stokes, speaker, coach, and author of *Cultural Competence Workbook*

"As a local church pastor, I want to finish well. I don't want to end up being a curmudgeonly old man who holds a grudge against the church and everyone who 'wronged' me. Neither do I want my wife and children to feel that way toward me or the church. So pick up this book and allow E. K. Strawser to be your guide away from that future. She will expose your assumptions and pastorally point you toward a beautiful kingdom vision of what sharing leadership in the church can look like."

Daniel Im, lead pastor at Beulah Alliance Church, podcaster, and author of *The Discipleship Opportunity: Leading a Great-Commission Church in a Post-Everything World*

"E. K. Strawser presents an honest assessment of broken hierarchical approaches to leadership and offers transformative principles to move today's ministry leader to a place of health and productivity. Strawser carefully guides the reader through a well-defined model of shared leadership that allows an honest look at how one leads and provides profound insight from professional and personal experiences that encourages accurate application of the Biblical texts on leadership. This book serves both as a necessary introduction to church leadership and a lifelong guide for leading well."

Kenneth R. Pruitt, president of Leland Seminary

"*You Were Never Meant to Lead Alone* delivers a timely truth for this cultural moment, and simultaneously, an ancient biblical truth that is rooted in Jesus and the early church. The wisdom, insight, and challenges shared on leadership in this book are grounded in real-life, hard-fought, fire-refined years of embodied leadership and renew my hope for the church, for the people of God, and for the body of Christ to be good news to a hurting world."

Rich Robinson, cofounder of Movement Leaders Collective and Creo and author of *All Change: Unlocking Kingdom Potential in a World We Weren't Prepared For*

"E. K. Strawser brilliantly reclaims shared leadership for the church, offering a vision where diverse gifts flourish and communities thrive together. With wisdom and practical insight, she equips leaders to dismantle hierarchy, embrace collaboration, and cultivate a church that truly reflects the body of Christ."

Sandra María Van Opstal, founder and executive director of Chasing Justice

"Believing in and practicing shared leadership in a power-hungry world (and, too often, a power-hungry church) is a prophetic act that proclaims a different kingdom and holds out hope in a final joy that is far better. E. K. Strawser not only teaches wonderfully and skillfully coaches us in this area of discipleship, so sorely needed in the church today, but she lives it and embodies it. Every church leadership that longs to be conformed to the way of Christ will find this book to be a healing balm and insightful guide."

Kyuboem Lee, professor of practical theology and doctor of ministry program director at Missio Seminary

"*You Were Never Meant to Lead Alone* is an important and inspiring book for our time, but it is not always easy to read. E. K. Strawser unflinchingly gets to the heart of some of our deepest dysfunctions within the Western church and calls them out. The joy of this book is that with stories, anecdotes, and a sense of playfulness and vision, she also sets out a biblical path to a healthy model for Apostles, Prophets, Evangelists, Shepherds, and Teachers (APEST) teamwork and communal leadership. Eun offers much-needed hope and practical advice to isolated leaders, pastors, and church communities looking for greater levels of health and maturity."
Paul Maconochie, director of Uptick

"In *You Were Never Meant to Lead Alone*, E. K. Strawser encourages us to not only see the beauty in shared leadership but the necessity for mature leaders who are equally mature followers. Her push for leaders that value all the gifts in our congregations and community is a refreshing reminder that powerful, transformative leadership may come from the least likely people. She reminds us that true empowerment comes when we recognize the power in diverse leadership styles and perspectives."
Jonathan "Pastah J" Brooks, lead pastor of Lawndale Christian Community Church and author of *Church Forsaken*

"*You Were Never Meant to Lead Alone* is a breath of fresh air for anyone in leadership. E. K. Strawser's authenticity shines as she blends her real-life journey with deep theological and practical insights. For too long, leadership models have exhausted and isolated us. Strawser offers a refreshing, communal approach, one modeled by generations, often by women, and now being shown as essential for the church. This timely book is for pastors, leaders recovering from burnout, and anyone striving to create transformative impact in their community by leading together."
Mozart Dixon Jr., vice president of planter services and strategic partnerships at Stadia

"This book is both a prophetic challenge and a pastoral companion for those in leadership. E. K. Strawser dismantles the myth of solo leadership and reimagines what it means to lead in authentic community. With a compelling blend of theology, personal story, and practical wisdom, she offers a road map for leaders who long to serve from a place of wholeness, shared responsibility, and Spirit-led collaboration. Looking for a healthier, more Christ-centered way forward? Let E. K. Strawser and this book be your guides!"
Lisa Rodriguez-Watson, national director of Missio Alliance

"Most leadership books leave individuals full of aspiration and devoid of meaningful vision for how to lead in community. In *You Were Never Meant to Lead Alone*, E. K. Strawser prunes our overgrown imaginations with practiced tools so that we can grow leadership fruit that tastes like the power of 'with.' This book will be an essential guide to help disciple generations of leaders to untether themselves from abusive systems that wreak havoc on their very souls."
Josh Hayden, author of *Remissioning Church*, pastor, and cofounder of 'Iwa Collaborative

"Leadership today requires a fresh approach that moves beyond traditional, top-down models. The complexities of our world demand leaders who are collaborative, inclusive, and adaptable. E. K. Strawser's *You Were Never Meant to Lead Alone* embodies this shift, advocating for shared leadership that values diverse gifts and perspectives. With practical insights and theological depth, Strawser empowers leaders to create stronger, more resilient teams, building ministries that reflect God's intention for the flourishing of the church and community."

Lorenzo A. Watson, CEO and president of the Christian Community Development Association

"With striking lucidity, E. K. Strawser diagnoses what ails much of the Western church today. This is no ordinary book on leadership. She gives voice to what I've struggled to articulate for years and offers insights I've simply not encountered elsewhere. If you're seeking an alternative to the dominant narratives of church leadership and growth, Strawser will lead you toward deeper formation, greater maturity, and a profoundly Christlike way of leading with others. This decolonized breath of fresh air is a must-read for every church leader!"

Kate Coleman, mentor, founding director of Next Leadership, and author of *Metamorph* and *7 Deadly Sins of Women in Leadership*

THE POWER OF
SHARING
LEADERSHIP

Y O U

WERE

NEVER

MEANT

TO

LEAD

ALONE

E. K. STRAWSER

FOREWORD BY ALEXIA SALVATIERRA
AFTERWORD BY DAVID E. FITCH

ivp

An imprint of InterVarsity Press
Downers Grove, Illinois

InterVarsity Press
P.O. Box 1400 | Downers Grove, IL 60515-1426
ivpress.com | email@ivpress.com

InterVarsity Press® is the publishing division of InterVarsity Christian Fellowship/USA®. For more information,
visit intervarsity.org.

All Scripture quotations, unless otherwise indicated, are taken from The Holy Bible, New International Version®, NIV®.
Copyright © 1973, 1978, 1984, 2011 by Biblica, Inc.™ Used by permission of Zondervan. All rights reserved worldwide.
www.zondervan.com. The "NIV" and "New International Version" are trademarks registered in the United States Patent
and Trademark Office by Biblica, Inc.™

While any stories in this book are true, some names and identifying information may have been changed to protect
the privacy of individuals.

The publisher cannot verify the accuracy or functionality of website URLs used in this book beyond the date
of publication.

Cover design: Faceout Studio, Spencer Fuller
Interior design: Daniel van Loon
Cover image: © CSA Images via Getty Images

ISBN 978-1-5140-1208-6 (print) | ISBN 978-1-5140-1209-3 (digital)

Printed in the United States of America ♾

Library of Congress Cataloging-in-Publication Data
A catalog record for this book is available from the Library of Congress.

32 31 30 29 28 27 26 25 | 13 12 11 10 9 8 7 6 5 4 3 2 1

To Melissa Wong and Hanzo Hamamura,

with whom I have experienced

the deepest level of both hope and lament in sharing leadership.

Aloha pumehana

CONTENTS

FOREWORD

ALEXIA SALVATIERRA

SINCE 2021, I HAVE SERVED as the academic dean of the Centro Latino of Fuller Theological Seminary, a fifty-year-old theological educational program for Spanish-speaking and bilingual students. One of the most challenging aspects of my job is to ensure that the seminary, historically structured to serve the dominant majority culture in the United States, serves our students well. This has meant advocating for translation in contexts where the expense for this service has never been budgeted and for higher general scholarship levels amid a widespread financial crisis.

While this is a frustrating process, it has also given birth to an important insight that I call the *choque*. The word *choque* in the Spanglish world is often used to refer to a car accident. The experience of running into the dominant culture's unconscious claim to universality creates the same set of physical and emotional reactions as a car accident—disorientation, confusion, pain, and shame. A natural impulse is to suppress the feelings, accept the current reality, and support the status quo. However, in that process, the particular potential contribution of the minority culture is lost—not only to its detriment but to the diminishment of the whole.

One of the most common *choques* that I encounter in my work is with a nexus of assumptions around individualism. I remember when a colleague with more experience in academia told me that I needed to write as an individual author, not with a team of coauthors, if I wanted to achieve tenure. I could not imagine why I would not write with a team, as the overall product would always be richer with the integration of different perspectives. When I explain my collective orientation, my colleagues almost always see the value of this vision and its corresponding skills. However, they often question how much value it contributes, whether the gain is worth the risk or the profit worth the loss. I have found that other minority leaders who experience a *choque* are often unwilling to fight for our perspectives to be valued and incorporated. Fighting for not only inclusion but equal recognition feels like a risk without much hope of reward.

When I read *You Were Never Meant to Lead Alone,* I wanted to stand up and cheer! Pastor Strawser is fearless, unflinching, and amazingly articulate in her case for a collective model of leadership that is both more faithful to the gospel and more effective for the twenty-first-century context. She also takes on another *choque*; she models being both bold and humble. She takes us through the detailed application of the model in her context while recognizing that no particular element is absolute. She admits that the APEST model (Apostles, Prophets, Evangelists, Shepherds, and Teachers) is limited and does not fully reflect reality, particularly in communities of color, but she makes a strong case for its utility. Her examples are not designed to inspire imitation but rather creativity and faith.

This is a necessary book for this kairos moment. May it midwife the change that the church needs for the sake of the world.

PROLOGUE

"EUN, YOU DO KNOW THAT THIS HASN'T HAPPENED *just* to you, right?" my therapist asked quietly.

I was tearful, asking her if there was something broken in me. How could another church leadership experience result in such a heavy degree of harm? Maybe I was doing something wrong? Or what if there was something inherently wrong with *me*.

Within just a few years' time, I was the first woman pastor to be invited into two different Christian institutional executive-leadership positions, one in a local church in the fastest-growing and largest denomination in my region and the second in an international church-planting organization, boasting over six hundred alumni church plants. Both were male-dominated spaces with two male executive-level leaders already in place. I was up for the challenge and excited about the chance to contribute. But when I raised some questions about leadership in either organization, I was met with drastic reactions. In the local church setting, I was once told, "If you don't follow what the leader says, then you're not obeying God." At another point, a top-tier leader told me to sign a letter of admission of absolute fault to protect a male co-leader—because it would "benefit the church." In the translocal setting, I was once told that all comments related to race and diversity must first go through one of the White male leaders before being brought up at any level of leadership. Another time, upon offering a grievance about workplace safety, I was told that I can either leave or conform.

My therapist gently brought me back from my grief and continued, "No, Eun. You're not alone in this." She proceeded to explain that, particularly as a woman pastor, a co-vocational pastor, an Asian American pastor, and an immigrant pastor, I share with many marginalized church leaders the experience of spiritual abuse, workplace inequities and attributional ambiguities, and both gender and racial discrimination. She then said the most striking thing: "Each of these methods of power in church leadership is a sin."

I needed to recognize some of the impacts of hierarchical church leadership as sin rather than dismiss them or make excuses for them: boys will be boys; churches will be churches. The three Hebrew words often translated as "sin" can help to clarify this: *khata, avon,* and *pesha. Khata* means "missing the goal"; *avon* best translates to "distorting what is good"; and *pesha* points to the consequences of "violating trust."[1] Outcomes of hierarchical church leadership are sinful when they have missed, distorted, or violated the trust of those they lead. Church leadership is about sharing leadership—how the first-century church exemplified leadership. Missiologists not only herald a sending God in the *missio Dei*; they also include the communal trinitarian God who shares leadership.[2]

I have endured pain both in hierarchical models of church leadership and in shared leadership. I will argue that hierarchical church leadership has so insidiously become the norm that it bleeds into the construct of shared leadership. When sharing leadership fails, it often isn't because sharing leadership doesn't work; it's because the church has once again participated in missing the goal, distorting what is good, and violating trust.

I also needed to recognize that I am not alone in this. My husband, Steve, and I, along with our three young adult and teenage kids, moved to Hawaii from West Philadelphia almost two decades ago. In the islands, I have often heard: "Another beautiful day in Hawai'i *nei*." I love that word *nei*. It translates to "this" or "here."[3] But it's more than that; it's a hyperlink to fill out the Hawaiian saying, *e ia nei*, which means, "You, beloved, who are here." When my therapist told me that I am not alone in *this*, I heard, *You, beloved, who are here, whose presence and lived story matter and take up actual space, are not alone.*

The most fruitful way that I have been utterly convinced of this *not-alone-ness* has been in hearing other leaders' stories of experiencing abuse and loss of power. I have heard the White woman pastor who was outcast from her own hometown because her initial congregation could not comprehend being led by a woman. Through grief and loss, she has regained her voice by joining with indigenous Native residents where she is a guest and now experiences the love of Creator God with them. I have heard the Black immigrant male pastor who, because his congregation was disenfranchised and disabled, couldn't even convince his White and Black peers ministering in the same city that he indeed pastored a real church. I have heard the Latina pastors who put their own reputations on the line in naming and challenging abuse of power from their Latino brothers, as if they broke a cultural code by "snitching." I have listened to the Korean American woman pastor who now leads a church that resides in a building once occupied by a Mars Hill megachurch, doing the repair and reparation work with the community that she does not bear guilt for. I have listened to the immigrant male pastor who was consistently seen as a second-class citizen at every level of leadership in which he has faithfully served, repeatedly being denied access, platform, and network.

Francis Weller, in conversation with Tim McKee, states,

> The work of the mature person is to carry grief in one hand and gratitude in the other and to be stretched large by them. How much sorrow can I hold? That's how much gratitude I can give. If I carry only grief, I'll bend toward cynicism and despair. If I have only gratitude, I'll become saccharine and won't develop much compassion for other people's suffering. Grief keeps the heart fluid and soft, which helps make compassion possible.[4]

Like so many of us in church leadership, I have learned the balance of carrying both grief and gratitude; it's the work of the mature church leader. I'd like to think I am a leader who's been stretched large and maintains the breakthrough possibility of Jesus' compassion with and for those he has given me to lead and love. I am instinctively and whole-heartedly committed to sharing leadership in the church. I don't really see it being done any other way. If the goal of the church's existence, its nondistorted image, and its trustworthiness are anchored on maturing together to be the communal reflection of Christ, then sharing leadership is what will equip it to be so. A church so equipped can contribute to the flourishing of the neighborhood, community, and city where it resides.

I've seen firsthand both the ugly parts of sharing leadership and the successful fulfillment of it. In my local church, Ma Ke Alo o (MKAO), which means "presence" in Hawaiian, we share leadership at every level of leadership. It's intentionally structured that way, built on a scaffolding formed over time. In fact, in six years' time, our church made the bold move from having one ordained lead pastor to three ordained lead pastors. Both of my now co-lead pastors, Meli and Hanzo, were hesitant at first and requested a rigorous process to become ordained. The process wasn't just about a skill set or theological know-how; it was filled with conversations and writing about commitment, character, capacity, calling, and community. They each wanted to do right by the congregation that was calling them. They also knew that they were being called to pastor a pioneering missional church that had raised up discipled and sent leaders. We started with one discipleship core of fifteen persons who participated in an open community dinner, ministering to about fifty persons each week in the first year. Now, seven years later, twelve different communities minister to over 650 persons, having multiplied to twenty-five leaders. Meli and Hanzo also wanted to do right by my leadership. They knew my journey of grief in church leadership.

Hanzo shared with me,

> Not that this actually helps with the things you went through, but I just need you to know how special you are to me and my family. I hope you can trust that I will never be one to screw you over. The ways that we are leading in MKAO are things I always hoped and dreamed the church could do, and you are at the spearhead of it. I'm in it with you for the long game, and I just need to say it from time to time.

Meli shared,

As time goes on, I grow ever more aware of how blessed I truly am to have you in my life. I honestly don't know where I would be if you didn't live a life that was so centered on discipleship. You are always the first to bestow and give honor away to others, but you are the one who I most honor and respect. Thank you for daily choosing to take the hard and narrow path for the sake of the kingdom and the flourishing of all those around you. I pray that God will give you peace and contentment in the work of your hands.

If Hanzo and Meli only knew how sharing church leadership with them has been a balm—not just to me in my own leadership but as a vision for our local church and churches everywhere. While my grief in church leadership runs deep, the gratitude I have in sharing leadership has stretched me and made me whole as a leader.

PART ONE

THE SHIFT FROM

HIERARCHICAL

LEADERSHIP

TO SHARING

LEADERSHIP

The Christian leader of the future is called to be completely irrelevant and to stand in this world with nothing to offer but his or her own vulnerable self.

HENRI NOUWEN

THE NATURE OF LEADERSHIP

*Leadership is one of the most complex and multidimensional phenomena.
It has been studied extensively over the years and has taken on greater
importance than ever before in today's fast-paced and increasingly
globalized world. Nonetheless, leadership continues to generate
captivating and confusing debate due to the complexity of the subject.*

SIHAME BENMIRA, MOYOSOLU AGBOOLA

*But Jesus called them together and said, "You know that the rulers
in this world lord it over their people, and officials flaunt their
authority over those under them. But among you it will be different.
Whoever wants to be a leader among you must be your servant."*

MATTHEW 20:25-26 NLT

THERE IS A THREE-PRONGED APPROACH to leadership in the
church in our day and age: lead until you become weary ("I'll sleep when
I'm dead"),[1] experience an insurmountable depth of loneliness ("It's lonely
at the top"),[2] and succeed by overpowering others. Weariness in church
leadership is an expected qualification of successful leadership that often
moves church leaders into experiencing loneliness and being tempted with
domineering power. Mark Driscoll, C. J. Mahaney, and Steve Timmis have
all succumbed to these pressures.[3]

"Leadership is lonely; welcome to the club!" Jason and Kai said to me,
bright eyed and sort of smiling. I was in a local coffee shop sitting across

from my two male pastor counterparts; it was the day before my ordination. I had hesitantly said yes to a co-leadership position in our local (and very successful) young church plant. After several years of our denomination's prodding, I only said yes after my youngest, who was about three at the time, slipped onto my lap during one church service and whispered into my ear, "Can girls be pastors?" Every leader she saw on the platform that day was male. I stepped into a leadership position because, first, I wanted to answer my daughter's question about women in leadership. Yes, we can. Second, I wanted to answer the question, Can leadership be shared? This church was about to give me that opportunity.

Church leadership, for women and men, is a lonely road. My two younger male counterparts, both in their early thirties, one White, the other Polynesian, had had no other paid work experience besides that of ministry. They were bright eyed and smiling because my acceptance of leadership would bring another person into their fold of commiserating on how life is so lonely at the top. "You'll be misunderstood," they said. "You can't have friends," they continued. Leadership is an isolating pathway, but worth it to advance God's kingdom. Or so they said.

It so happened that Jason and Kai also came out of an all-too-familiar leadership structure: working with a senior pastor—a tall, thick, bravado of a Latino pastor, highly regarded in the denomination—who regularly told the church about his beautiful, sexy wife and raised up only male leaders in an egalitarian denomination. He was infamously known for his strong-handed leadership, spending most of the weekly staff meetings issuing orders, criticizing mistakes, and shooting down anyone else's feedback. It was said of Pastor Juan that he spoke the words of God, and if you didn't accept what he said, then you were rejecting the voice of God. I've known a series of young men who could not weather this senior pastor's storm, but Jason and Kai had. And what was their reward? To lead a church of their own. Domineering leadership like this is often seen as a strength and something to endure, be loyal to, and learn from. Because of this, domineering leadership in the church is reproduced repeatedly.

Amid recurring news of domineering church leadership and failure of church leadership, most efforts to devise an antidote to this toxic leadership culture in the church have focused on the psychological health, soul care, and better sabbath techniques for the burned-out main leader. Fix the leader, heal the leader, or train the leader. It has left an extensive wake of communal harm, confusion, and grief. A better leadership model is needed to replace weary, lonely, and domineering leadership in the church. There is also a need to contribute a practical real-life model of sharing leadership for the church today and a lived-out model that includes both women and men, BIPOC (Black, Indigenous, and People of Color) leaders, and the local cultural community.

Whether we like to admit it or not, history and culture, tradition and systems, shape so much of what we expect in leadership, both for persons who hold a leadership position and for people who appoint people to those positions.

EXPECTATIONS SHAPE THE LEADER

Warren Bennis states that "leadership is the most studied and least understood topic of any in the social sciences." He continues, "Never have so many labored so long to say so little."[4] While the debate on what makes a good leader goes from "great leaders are born"[5] to "great leaders are made,"[6] we are left unsettled. In a global world where leadership decisions affect the daily lives of so many people, we are often left feeling helpless in a changing world. Unfortunately, we routinely see headlines of failed leadership these days.

Leadership impacts all of us, and yet it is so misunderstood or poorly understood. As a senior pastor for a local church here in Hawaii, I think the sentiment is more pronounced when it comes to church leadership.

On one hand, the intrinsic perspective of leadership, that "great leaders are born," has an additional nuance for the church leader. The traits required for church leadership are not just those that move a person to action, as is the case for most secular leadership positions (including business leaders, nonprofit administrators, and politicians). The required leadership traits must showcase an intrinsic morality. Nearly 65 percent of Christians in the United States say that the most important trait for a Christian leader is integrity, followed by authenticity. The least listed traits are passion for God, humility, and purpose.[7]

When I hear *integrity* in a predominantly American White evangelical Christian context, I picture an uncompromising adherence to a White evangelical portrait of Jesus. While integrity often looks like a person who is the same in all situations with all people, the integrity that the congregation often wants is a pastor who has uncompromising adherence to their moral viewpoint. Unchanging, inflexible. And when I hear *authenticity*, I hear a demand from a congregation worshiping its own privatized religion that the leader be "relatable" (meaning, make me feel personally comfortable). Because of the identity of those who promote "The Great Man" theory, it already connotes that women are excluded from leadership.

In stark contrast to the great (Christian) man theory, the extrinsic perspective of church leadership, that "great leaders are made," suggests that if anyone were to commit to certain skill sets, over time that person could lead the church too. Perhaps a framework could be devised that includes Christian formation, personal formation, relational skills, intellectual skills, and management skills.[8] Then you could be a pastor too! This seems to minimize the sense of call that most church leaders, both women and men, have experienced in making the courageous decision to lead, matched by discernment from the Jesus community calling them to lead.

In my current local context, I am a co-vocational founding pastor of a missional community–based church plant in Hawaii. In our seventh year we have multiplied from one community to twelve, serving the needs of over 650 persons. I have equipped over twenty-five missional community leaders who tethered their discipleship to community renewal. In my previous church leadership context, I was one of three executive team pastors in the fastest-growing and largest denomination in the state, the only woman pastor at this level of leadership in Hawaii. During my time in this position, we grew our church-plant team of twenty volunteers to 450 Sunday worship service attendees in five years' time, with 80 percent of our worship attendees participating in these missional community groups. I equipped eighty-five community leaders, who tethered their discipleship to community renewal and cultivated a communal discipleship model that produced over a hundred active disciples in six months' time. What's more, I have served on an executive leadership team (three persons) for an international church-planting training organization with over six hundred alumni around the world. In addition, I manage my own consulting firm, working with church plants, established churches, denominations, seminaries, and Christian community-development nonprofits on centering discipleship and moving their people through change processes. I am a physician by trade, own my own practice, am a published author, and contribute to professional journals. I am routinely asked to sit on governing boards of local and translocal institutions, have been married to Steve for twenty-two years, raised three insanely thoughtful and kind children, care for my elderly parents, graduated from an Ivy League institution, and am a Fulbright Scholar.

Pretty impressive resumé, huh? Not to mention I have a third-degree black belt in Tang Soo Do. I am a direct descendant of King Sejong Lee in Korea (the guy who invented the Korean alphabet and brought literacy to the Korean people), the only daughter of a decorated colonel who fought in the Vietnam War, play the piano, and taught both Swahili and medicine in higher education.

I resonate deeply with the apostle Paul when he writes to the Jesus communities in Philippi:

> If someone else thinks they have reasons to put confidence in the flesh, I have more: circumcised on the eighth day, of the people of Israel, of the tribe of Benjamin, a Hebrew of Hebrews; in regard to the law, a Pharisee; as for zeal, persecuting the church; as for righteousness based on the law, faultless.
>
> But whatever were gains to me I now consider loss for the sake of Christ. (Phil 3:4-7)

I resonate deeply with him because none of my "reasons to put confidence in the flesh" capture whether I'm a good leader. They don't even capture if I follow Jesus.

THE ANATOMY OF A CHURCH LEADER

Just as there are numerous studies on the complexities of leadership in social science, there are numerous conversations about the complexities of church leadership. There are a few things to keep in mind as we consider teasing apart what makes a church leader. First, when speaking about church leadership, the dominant culture of the Western church—that is, the White evangelical church—is the loudest voice in both literary and conversational contributions. That being said, we need to keep in mind that the loudest voice is not always the most correct voice. It may only indicate which churches and church leaders have more access to resources, funding, time, network relationships, and opportunity. There is a skewed lack of voices from immigrant church leaders, BIPOC church leaders, and women church leaders. Second, church leadership has historically (and still today) rendered so much personal and communal hurt. We have to keep in mind that stories of failed leadership are not just about the leaders' mistakes; these stories also describe broken communities in the leaders' wake. Third, the most prominent leadership structure still used today is hierarchical leadership, and in the church this draws less from hierarchy in business structures and more from social hierarchy. Hierarchy isn't just a leadership structure; it's a power structure. Isabel Wilkerson, the first African American woman to win the Pulitzer Prize in journalism, writes about social hierarchy:

> Caste [or our current social hierarchical ladder] is insidious and therefore powerful because it is not hatred, it is not necessarily personal. It is the worn grooves of comforting routes and unthinking expectations, spatters of a social order that have been in place for so long that it looks like the natural order of things.[9]

The picture of the Western church leader is a skewed and colonized image, a leader who has participated in a history of communal damage and holds a position of great power and authority. Ultimately, the church leader is not dealing with structures and organizations or decision-making and management; the church leader in our modern time must reckon with power.

LEADERSHIP IN THE FIRST-CENTURY CHURCH

Nijay Gupta writes, "When we read the New Testament, especially Acts and the Epistles, we get the impression that the early Christians intentionally avoided the pyramid leadership system, certainly rejecting any kind of human 'ruler' of churches,"[10] consciously rejecting authoritarian systems that were prevalent in their contemporary Roman society. The pyramid structure of leadership, or hierarchical structure of leadership as it is more popularly called today, was not the model early Christians wished for their leadership structure. As Gupta notes,

> Roman people prized social class. At the top of the pyramid you had the emperor, of course, the highest person in the land. Below that you had the senatorial class, a tier of nobles with considerable wealth and political power. Then the equestrian class, a rank of wealth, men hoping to rise up into the senatorial echelon. Underneath that you had commoners, then foreigners, then freedpersons (ex-slaves), and last of all slaves.[11]

In the norm-disrupting culture of the first-century church, the center of their communal life was table fellowship, and all social class was disrupted at the table.[12] As Paul writes to the Jesus communities in Galatia, "So in Christ Jesus you are all children of God through faith, for all of you who were baptized into Christ have clothed yourselves with Christ. There is neither Jew nor Gentile, neither slave nor free, nor is there male and female, for you are all one in Christ Jesus" (Gal 3:26-28).

In the first-century church, there was no hierarchical leadership structure. On the other hand, there was no flat leadership structure either. In the business world, a flat organization has no management levels between the employees and their employer, the idea being that it decreases budget cost for middle management while increasing the staff's involvement in decision-making and independence. The biggest downside is that there's "a risk for generalization and confusion if the company fails to hone and specifically direct team goals and talents."[13] Too many decision makers, no decisions made. Flat leadership structure in the modern church often results from resistance to our current dominant hierarchical church leadership structure—a resistance to reliance on a single decision maker.

Gupta highlights that in the first-century church the ethos of leadership centered on the community rather than instruction or worship. For the most part, each of apostle Paul's letters to the Jesus communities was addressed to the whole congregation. The community listened together. "Paul's tendency was to refer to leadership as giving care and oversight, not wielding power and authority."[14] Soong-Chan Rah adds in *The Next Evangelicalism*, "Acts 2 points to an evangelism and church growth that incorporates the secondary cultural system of the preached word with the primary cultural system of self-sacrificial living."[15] Further evidence that the emphasis of the first-century church was not on instruction or worship but on community. For most of the churches across the Greco-Roman world, Jesus communities met together in homes, and leadership was provided by both women and men as ministry/care providers (*diakonos*) and overseers/managers (*episkopos*).[16]

In the first-century church, all participated, but there was no flat leadership structure. Instead, oversight or care was provided by more senior or seasoned leaders. Therefore, I would argue that in the first-century church leadership was shared.

SHARING LEADERSHIP

Not only is sharing leadership the vital antidote to the "great man" and "great skills" theories (and presumptions) of leadership, but this approach is foundational for addressing the severity of weariness, loneliness, and domineering leadership in the church today. Sharing leadership in the church is not just a good idea; sharing leadership is essential to the flourishing of both the church and the community the church resides in. It's not just a nice picture of what the church could experience; it's the very portrait of ideal leadership as it was intended for the church.

The remainder of part one will address the idea that leadership is not about a skill set or intrinsic traits; leadership is about maturity. I will identify the marks of maturity in leadership and demonstrate how progression in maturity requires sharing leadership. Part two will explore a commonly used fivefold leadership delineation from Ephesians 4—Apostles, Prophets, Evangelists, Shepherds, and Teachers (APEST)—as a tool for framing sharing leadership with the clear goal of equipping the church. The principles of APEST will be applied to all types of leaders, especially addressing gender, race, and culture. Part three will consider the practicals: how to identify sharing leaders, structure sharing leadership in the church, and sustain sharing leadership.

HŌKŪLE'A

In *Hawaiki Rising*, Sam Low writes passionately and reverently about the *Hōkūle'a*, the voyaging canoe led by legendary navigator Nainoa Thompson, which by now has traveled over 150,000 miles of clear Pacifica guided by star navigation.[17] The first *Hōkūle'a* voyage in 1975 occurred during a time when the people of Hawaii were experiencing a generation of lost heritage. Most of the young adults at that time grew up never having seen authentic hula (traditional Hawaiian ceremonial dance), heard traditional *mele* (song), or spoken 'Ōlelo Hawai'i (Hawaiian language). In the late 1800s, the independent Hawaiian kingdom was overthrown by the United States. Act 57, sec. 30, of the 1896 Laws of the Republic of Hawaii mandated that English become the only medium of instruction throughout Hawaii and prohibited the use of the Hawaiian language in schools, a rule reinforced with corporal punishment.[18] The same mandate prohibited hula, *mele*, and traditional ceremony. Nainoa Thompson's maiden voyage on *Hōkūle'a*, re-learning how to navigate by the stars in open ocean like thousands of his indigenous Hawaiians' ancestors, occurred during what is now called the Hawaiian cultural revolution.

To celebrate the heritage of Hawaii, my husband, Steve, and I went to our kids' elementary school early and signed them out. "What are we doing?" asked Beren, our oldest and a very studious eight-year-old at the time. Emma, our middle child, a kindergartner, then exclaimed, "Yay! We're getting out early!" Kyriella, the baby, having just turned four a few days prior, was wide-eyed and excited to see her older siblings so early. We ran down to the beach and joined a quickly forming throng of people on shore. Without hesitation, the five of us swam out to the *Hōkūleʻa*. The canoe was about to embark on another voyage, and before it launched, it was making some key stops across all the Hawaiian Islands. We swam with our little ones and got hoisted on board. The navigators, so kind and warm, let the kids tinker with navigation tools and showed them around the large *waʻa kaulua* (double-hulled canoe), where they fished, where they slept, and where they navigated. Then the five of us, on the count of three, jumped off the *Hōkūleʻa* together. (Beren was timid but reassured, Emma was squealing with joy, and Kyriella just held onto Steve and then asked to do it again.) We're transplants from Philadelphia, but we were brimming with reverence because we knew just how much the *Hōkūleʻa* meant for the people and the islands that we have come to love.

When I pray for the kingdom of God to come to Hawaii, I always get an image of the *Hōkūleʻa*. I see the double-hulled canoe approaching the shores slowly but surely, with such an air of regal reverence. I see an endless multitude of people waiting at the shoreline, pining to get a glimpse of it, overjoyed at its arrival. Everyone waiting at the beach knew what it was; the kingdom of God was at hand, and everyone could recognize it because it was coming as something recognizable to them.

Sharing leadership is vital to my own leadership. It's vital to my leadership because I lead in a local Hawaiian context that isn't my own. I lead a community of mostly locally born and raised-in-Hawaii people. My participation in the existing work of God in Hawaii has nothing to do with my abilities or accomplishments; it has everything to do with the ones with whom I share power. While I started as the solo lead pastor with my congregation expecting that I would lead alone, it was never my intention to remain alone. It's essential that I share power, especially with a culture of people who have lost so much of their identity and purpose to White Christian colonization. How I share leadership with my people is vital for them to recognize that the kingdom of God is at hand in their place and that they are fully invited to join in.

I'm not a good leader because of my CV. I know I'm a good leader because my local leaders let me know. Marissa, one of our local church leaders, Maui-born and raised, educator, lover of her islands and her people, happiest when waist deep in a *lo'i kalo* (taro patch) and sharing the beauty and richness of her culture with others, told me,

> When praying for you, *pikake* was the word I kept hearing and the fragrance I kept smelling. *Pikake* is adapted from the word *peacock* because Princess Ka'iulani[19] was fond of both the bird and flower. The *pikake* is normally worn by women during ceremonies and rituals to honor the person. It felt fitting to adorn you with the *pikake*. I want to honor the work that you've done and are doing, the leader that you are. Like Princess Ka'iulani, you demonstrate a life of strength and compassion for your people and because of your people.

2

SHARING LEADERSHIP REQUIRES MATURITY

The true measure of leadership is not the authority you command or the number of followers you have. Your success as a leader is how much good people do thanks to your presence. Your legacy as a leader is how much good people keep doing in your absence.

ADAM GRANT

Remember your leaders, who spoke the word of God to you. Consider the outcome of their way of life and imitate their faith.

HEBREWS 13:7

"MR. AND MRS. STRAWSER, your daughter has leadership qualities." It's probably what every parent would be pining to hear at a parent-teacher conference, and this came from an educator who spent extended time during my first grader's waking hours gaining insight and observing how she operates. While it thrilled me to hear this positive report from the teacher, I asked, "Oh, how do you see leadership qualities in Kyriella?" I also asked because Kyriella is our youngest of three, and we had heard this report about her siblings when they were in first grade. With each kid, the teacher identified a different trait that led her to believe that each child had leadership qualities. Beren, our oldest, is the quintessential oldest son, who has a deep sense of morality and of right and wrong ways of doing things.

His ability to accomplish assignments and answer all the questions with compliance and speed convinced his teacher that he was a natural-born leader. Emma, our middle child, lover-of-life daughter, exudes compassion and is a hugger. Her ability to welcome new students and be noticeably enthusiastic in class led her teacher to believe she was a natural-born leader. At the parent-teacher conference for Kyriella in first grade, we once again heard that she was a natural-born leader. Our youngest was known to be a little "bossy," but her dimples allowed her to take command of any group project without hurt feelings. "A natural-born leader!"

What are the traits that we look for in people that informs us that they are "natural-born" leaders? How do we know that certain people are the leaders to whom we should give our consent, or listen to, or follow after? Should other students follow Beren because he can answer all the questions? Or Emma because she's happy and likable? Or Kyriella because she's a little bossy?

"Leadership is one of those 'if you see it, you know it' kind of qualities," writes David Kinnaman from Barna Group. The study continues, "More than eight in ten (82%) Christians believe the United States is facing a crisis of leadership because there aren't enough leaders."[1] In addition to this, nearly 90 percent of US adults do not find church leaders to be credible when it comes to important issues of our day. In fact, most leaders only believe they have none to some influence even within their own congregations.[2] There is an inexplicable decline in the church in both leaders and their impact. Furthermore, when we account for the emerging generations of millennials and Generation Z, who are looking for traits of collaboration, purposefulness, and humility in those they are willing to follow, we must recognize that they

> have grown up in the most diverse generations the U.S. has seen thus far. They are also connected to their peers around the world and are highly aware of the social issues that plague not just our country, but nations around the globe. When it comes to solutions for these issues however, young people are not turning to the Church for answers.[3]

Generation X and boomers desire a pastor who greets us, knows us and our family by name, preaches the gospel we are familiar with, visits us when we're sick, and meets our congregational needs. Millennials and Generation Z desire a pastor who is in fashion and current on trends, engaging both on and off stage, and up to speed with social issues concerning both politics and justice. It seems the church today calls for a leader who is most like them and not necessarily most like Christ.

TYPES OF AUTHORITY

Leadership often feels culture dependent. It arises from the cultural perspective of giving power over to those who can wield control, gather a crowd, or yield successful contribution.

The person in the room who appears to be in control, is maintaining control, or has the most self-control is often treated as the leader. And the person who has control is the person who is making decisions. People assume that those who are able to make decisions (and often clearly, quickly, and measured) are competent leaders. Leadership through control is connected to decision-making authority.

The person in the room who appears to be able to gather the largest crowd around them, whether by their personality, physical attractiveness, or unique abilities, also is often treated as the leader. People assume that those who are able to gather large groups of people have leadership qualities. And the person who has crowd-sourcing prowess is connected to influence. Leadership through crowds is connected to relational authority.

The person in the room who appears to have had the most experience, credibility, and expertise is also often treated as the leader. And the person who has the most accomplished resumé and the longest list of proficiencies appears to be most qualified to lead. Leadership through contribution is connected to accomplishment-based authority.

Without a second thought, we tend to give authoritative and leadership power to those who present with competence, influence, and experience. We don't often pause to think that sometimes being able to make decisions is more about the privilege and personality it takes to gain access to power, or that popularity comes from the ability to meet entertainment and pleasure needs over character and content that may be convicting and confrontational, or that degrees, years, and accomplishments may not equate to a person's proficiency in leading in all matters.

Christ was patient, compassionate, and interruptible when making decisions (Mk 5:25-34). He often avoided crowds (Lk 5:15-16) and did not rule over anyone even though he was God (Mt 20:25-29). Even his hand-picked disciples and earliest followers were mostly women and men who did not hold outright societal competence, influence, or expertise. They did not hold decision-making, relational, or accomplishment-based authority of any kind, particularly in an empire-occupied land. And yet, Jesus describes these people with power words, as those who will inherit the kingdom of God and have proximity to God (Mt 5:1-12).

Our post-modern/post-Christian culture celebrates leadership gained through control, crowd, and contribution. We judge leadership as though conducting a casting call rather than basing it on a list of capabilities or character. In the business world, we often deny promotions to those who increase the bottom line jointly with their colleagues or show perseverance and professionalism in pressured situations. Instead, we move people into higher management positions because of their likable or competitive personality and call it compatibility.[4] In the political arena, we choose candidates not by their values, how collaborative they are across party lines, or how well they listen to a diverse set of constituents but by our perception of their personality. That is, I want my leaders to look like me. While Congress has experienced an incremental increase in racial, gender, and age diversity, our recent lawmakers were 99 percent male, White, cis, middle-aged, tall, able-bodied, experienced in the military, educated, and well spoken.[5] We think better educators are those who are more attractive and amusing than those who are more nurturing and formative.[6] Doling out leadership via the lens of control, crowd, and contribution is everywhere. And these values have seeped into choices for church leadership as well.

POWER PRESSURES OF LEADERSHIP

In the church, we may not use the same vocabulary, but we measure a person's ability to lead by how competent they are, and people who seem to be in control or command control appear to be competent. We judge that a competent person must be able to make decisions. Those who are able to draw and engage a crowd appear to be influential. And influence suggests that a person is able to sway and carry a higher relational network. Those who have a list of experiences and expertise appear to have proven their contribution. And people with experience and expertise are accomplished enough to have the final say. When a church is calling a new senior pastor, most often we choose our leaders from those who appear to command control, draw a crowd, or have proven their contribution.

I've been a part of Christian organizations in which the leader commanded much control, which seemed to build a quick and clear direction forward. But in the end, his (and usually it is a man) domineering and loud control silenced everyone else's voices and facilitated abuse of power. I've been in congregations where we were excited about a dynamic new senior pastor who drew in large crowds of people on a Sunday morning but learned that he was having an illicit relationship with an elder. I've also participated in ministry teams who risked no innovation because the main leader was convinced that he had the most experience and therefore the most expertise to keep things the same, despite decline and eventual closure.

Leadership without self-examination of the motivation for desiring to lead is poor and stagnant at best and dangerous and harmful at worst. But, before we uncover our underlying desires within leadership, we'll look at the unique power pressures that come with leading in the church (see table 2.1).

There are two unique power pressures in pastoring a church: the pressure to meet communal expectations and the pressure for church growth. There is no other profession that puts this kind of pressure on a leader.

Table 2.1. Unique power pressures in pastoring a church

Unique power pressures	What the congregation wants	What the congregation expects from the pastor	What the congregation does NOT want from the pastor
Communal expectations	Ideal community	Social availability	Challenge
Church growth	Increased attendance	Sermons	Change

For the most part, the hiring and firing of pastors are determined by social availability to the congregation and growth of the congregation based on the singular tool of preaching. The social connection is often not mutually reciprocated, and there must be no sense of challenge to the status quo, which leads to both a severe sense of isolation in the leader and a decrease in meaningful impact within the congregation and most importantly throughout the community.[7] Growth or flourishing of the church is measured mainly by how many people attend the weekly Sunday services and contribute to the offering plate and by whether the building has either heat or air conditioning. Soong-Chan Rah, professor of evangelism at Fuller Theological Seminary, states,

> How do we measure "success" in the typical American church—by the standards of Scripture or by the standards of the American consumer value system? Typically, we will see the success of churches measured by the numerical size of the church and the financial health of the church (oftentimes reflected in the condition and appearance of the church building). In more colloquial language, we focus on the ABCs of church success: Attendance, Buildings and Cash. Or even more directly, the three Bs of church success: Building, Bucks and Butts. The church holds the same materialistic values held by American society. We measure success in the church with standards as worldly as the most secular Fortune 500 company. Churches are no more than businesses (albeit nonprofit ones) with the bottom line being the number of attendees or the size of the church budget. American evangelicalism is held captive to the materialistic and consumeristic values of American society.[8]

Jay Kim, lead pastor of WestGate Church in Silicon Valley, says, "Unfortunately, the underlying forces driving some church searches are the basic tenets of individualistic consumerism, born out of an assumption that 'church' is primarily a product package of goods and services, designed and marketed to achieve customer satisfaction."[9] Which church is the most comfortable? Agreeable? Entertaining? In other words, which church makes me feel the least uncomfortable, supports my viewpoints and opinions, and grabs my attention? Which pastor provides me with personal comfort, personal support, and personal amusement? The platformed church leaders today are either caring leaders, charismatic leaders, or clever leaders. Congregants church shop seeking a father (or mother) figure, a popular and entertaining leader, or a scripturally knowledgeable leader.[10]

The pressure to provide a certain kind of worship service and sermon each week to achieve an increase in attendance is a job description fit for Sisyphus. In addition to that impossible responsibility, pastors must navigate the sensitive nature of congregants who have a deep expectation for community. Dietrich Bonhoeffer writes that "those who love their dream of a Christian community more than the Christian community itself become destroyers of that Christian community even though their personal intentions may be ever so honest, earnest, and sacrificial."[11] The pastor's impossible job is to meet the congregation's demand for consumerism and an ideal social club.

UNDERLYING DESIRES OF LEADERSHIP IN THE CHURCH

Therefore, it goes without saying that the unique pressures placed on a pastor (the underlying desires the church has for its leadership) are intricately entwined with the pastor's own motivations for leadership.

In order to examine our underlying desires in leadership, it's important to humbly and honestly uncover our motivation for why we lead, why we lead in the manner we adopt, why we are leading this congregation, and why we are leading in this community. Do I lead because I want to be liked? Do I lead because I want to accomplish something? Do I lead because I want to be in control? While the different types of authority (decision-making, relational, and accomplishment-based) are neutral and serve as conduits for leadership, each can reveal an underlying motivation that may not be as innocent as we think.

Power, popularity, and productivity are underlying desires that are often encouraged in church leaders, but they can subversively shape how leadership makes decisions and what leaders value. Sadly, we have seen how these underlying desires for command, fame, and a sense of accomplishment have devastated many congregations, with prominent leaders engaging in abuse of oppressive power, manipulative relational power, and unchecked power.[12]

We can also see that out of these underlying leadership desires, a specific kind of community is formed. With a desire for power, we produce a community of people who are disempowered. With a desire for popularity, we produce a community of people who are dependent. And with a desire for productivity, we produce a community of people who are performative.

What the leader desires will almost always shape the community, whether the leader is aware of it or not. Let me be clear: the leadership traits of being able to effectively wield control (competence), crowd (influence), and contribution (expertise) are not the issue. The leader must address the underlying desires that come with leadership (see table 2.2). The desire for power values control and therefore leaves the community devoid of their own voice or seat at the decision-making table. The desire for popularity cherishes being liked by the crowd and therefore leaves the community relationally dependent on the leader and not on one another. The desire for productivity esteems the completion of tasks and therefore leaves the community deprived of rest and relationship.

Table 2.2. Underlying desires of the leader

Leadership trait	Type of authority	Underlying desire
Control	Decision-making (competence)	Power
Crowd	Relational (influence)	Popularity
Contribution	Accomplishment (expertise)	Productivity

We find ourselves bouncing between just two offerings of leadership: dominant or dynamic leaders. On one hand, we want leaders who command and present decisiveness; their authoritativeness offers us comfort because they have everything under control. On the other hand, we want leaders who are admirable and inspiring; their prestige offers us proximity to influence. Borrowing from psychology and its evolutionary theory of leadership emergence, dominance and dynamism (authority and prestige) are the dual routes to leadership.[13] We often believe that those who reassure us by providing the control that we lack (dominant leadership) or those who offer us power when we lack confidence (dynamic leadership) are the kinds of leaders we need (see table 2.3). We so easily give over leadership to those who make us feel safe or special.

Table 2.3. Dominant or dynamic leadership types

Leadership type	Movement of power	Proximity to	Felt need	How follower feels
Dominant	Power over others	Control/ authority	Lack of personal control	Safe
Dynamic	Power provided to others	Influence/ prestige	Lack of personal confidence	Special

The relationship between what church leaders desire and what church congregants desire is a tension-filled progression, so often involving personal needs and expectations. Because needs (meaning felt needs over basic needs) and expectations (meaning idealized over pragmatic) based on desire are usually unnamed, this elevated tension is established without self-reflection. However, desire exposes our values. Ultimately, we as church leaders desire and value power, popularity, and productivity; our congregation desires and values feeling safe and special.

Pastor D., the senior pastor and founder of his church has also been the main teaching pastor for the twenty years of the church's existence. Recently, he has encountered some physical limitations and has had a difficult time transferring authority to others. While making a name for himself as the authoritative biblical voice in his region, hosting invitation-only preaching clubs for other male pastors across denominations, he is left with a congregation that has become so dependent on his teachings that sharing the pulpit has proven difficult. Expertise alone does not mark a good church leader, and it discourages sharing leadership.

Pastor K., the senior pastor who founded his church ten years ago, recently closed his church after choosing to move in another direction. He had been able to draw a crowd of a hundred millennial and Gen Z, artsy, and athletic congregants week after week with his surfer vibe and relatable messages. Despite having some second-tier leadership in place, he decided to close up shop, leaving a hundred displaced people with only a month's notice. Influence alone does not mark a good church leader, and it seldom allows shared leadership.

Pastor C. is a senior pastor who helped start his church two decades ago. He spent most of his time mentoring young men to step into church leadership, handpicking his church council members, often running a tight ship in meetings, and imposing direction and vision without question. Twenty years later, and he has yet to pass off senior-level leadership to the men he has mentored, though he has not provided for preaching, pastoral care, or administrative care for the church. Control alone does not mark a good church leader, and it most often prevents sharing leadership.

A clear marker for immature leadership is the desire not to share leadership.

SHARING LEADERSHIP REQUIRES MATURITY

Where do we go with this?

What is the alternative to deep motivation for power, popularity, and productivity, that is, to have control, to be liked, and to accomplish? What motivation can be identified that tells us without a shadow of a doubt that a leader is called to lead? And what kind of impact would such a leader have on a community?

Without self-examination, we would inevitably think that those who are the most capable of gaining control, gathering a crowd, or contributing the most are the most mature leaders in the community. Leadership does often require these qualities, so this is not about erasing these key pieces of leadership development. But, what if maturity in leadership required different motivations? If maturity were to be about progressively growing into a leader who is more like Christ, then maturity ought to examine the motivations of Christ.

All three Synoptic Gospels describe the temptation of Christ while in the wilderness for forty days and nights following his baptism (Mt 4:1-11; Mk 1:12-13; Lk 4:1-13). Immediately after he hears from the Father, "This is my Son, whom I love; with him I am well pleased" (Mt 3:17), Jesus is confronted with "*If* you are the Son of God . . ." (Mt 4:3, 6, italics added). Ultimately, contending with our underlying leadership desires is about addressing our identity. Leaders who imitate Jesus are leaders who are gradually rooting their identity deeper in Christ and farther from desiring power, popularity, and productivity.

We would be leaders who imitate Jesus in how we interact with making decisions, having influence, and what we do with our experience and expertise. We would be leaders who do our leading after first hearing, "You are my child, whom I love; with you I am well pleased." Doing the hard work of addressing our identity as leaders requires us to contend with power. Jesus contended with power, and he shared it.

3

MATURE LEADERS ARE DISCIPLES FIRST

I tell my students, "When you get these jobs that you have been so brilliantly trained for, just remember that your real job is that if you are free, you need to free somebody else. If you have some power, then your job is to empower somebody else. This is not just a grab-bag candy game."

TONI MORRISON

And whoever wants to be first must be your slave—just as the Son of Man did not come to be served, but to serve, and to give his life as a ransom for many.

MATTHEW 20:27-28

WE HAVE A GIGANTIC HADEN MANGO TREE in our backyard. It has hosted many children climbing and sitting on its branches. Java sparrows love to nest in it. Its branches span about sixty feet, and it rises sixty feet tall. It's massive. The previous owners boasted that the tree produces three hundred mangoes each year. They didn't lie. For many years we harvested so many mangoes that we would host mango-picking parties in the backyard, and everyone left with a bag of bright red and yellow mangoes. Hawaii's gold. But after a particularly stormy winter, we knew that we had to get the tree pruned. Now, when you prune a giant mango tree, you have to hire a professional tree trimmer and an arborist to determine the health of the tree. Our tree is so colossal that it took three different, heavily involved operations with lifts and ropes and machinery to cut the tree. Three prunings. The following year, we had a total of zero mangoes during mango season. Zero. The year after that, none. For five years, our old mango tree did not produce any fruit.

Jesus tells his disciples in John 15, "I am the true vine, and my Father is the gardener. He cuts off every branch in me that bears no fruit, while every branch that does bear fruit he prunes so that it will be even more fruitful" (Jn 15:1-2). Pruning is a maturing process for a tree, though it seems like an odd process for growth because it involves cutting off. But the purpose of pruning is to remove an already fruiting branch to make the tree even more fruitful. The process of maturing means to be "even more fruitful." If you're not even more fruitful, then you're not maturing.

Our mango tree that had been bearing three hundred mangoes a season, once pruned, did not bear fruit for five years. But then it happened. Our mango tree now produces a thousand of the largest, brightest, sun-hued mangoes. Our mango tree is maturing, and we know this because it is even more fruitful.

We are in desperate need of leaders who are maturing. We are in desperate need of leaders who are even more fruitful. But what does being fruitful as a leader mean?

LEADERSHIP REQUIRES MATURITY

Leadership requires maturity, but our current cultural context shapes what leaders desire in their own leadership (wanting power, popularity, or productivity) and what the congregation desires from their leaders (feeling safe or special). There is a unique pressure placed on contemporary church leaders in having to meet the expectations for an ideal community through social availability (without challenge) and church growth through sermons (without change).

To clarify what maturity in leadership looks like in the church, we need to address a few threads. First, we'll look at the unique pressures for church growth and the establishment of an ideal community. Second, we'll move into the importance of discipleship in the life of the leader. Last, we'll land on the marks of maturity in leadership.

HOW MATURE LEADERS ADDRESS POWER PRESSURES

When Christian leaders state that they long to go back to the "Acts 2 church," most are not referencing a longing to plant a church amid political turmoil, cultural minority, and religious persecution. They are referencing Acts 2:41, "Those who accepted his message were baptized, and about three thousand were added to their number that day." Most modern readers (and particularly church leaders) attribute the great crowd's salvation to Peter's sermon (Acts 2:14-39). In response, they think, "Three thousand people came to the front when Peter gave the altar call after his inspiring sermon. Therefore, to increase numerical church growth, I have to give an inspiring sermon." And church members believe that for a church to grow, the pastor needs to give inspiring sermons.

Robert Linthicum responds to this desire for church growth:

> I know of no instrument [church attendance statistics] that creates more guilt and sense of failure in my denomination than this instrument. That is because it favors any church located in a community of rapid growth and radically disfavors any church in a decaying, declining community. The first kind of community is found mostly in suburban areas of the United States, while the second is found primarily in inner cities.[1]

Yet, as biblical scholar Nils Lund contributes, if we were to read Acts 2 as a first-century Christian, we would immediately focus on the architecture of the passage. Luke uses a chiastic structure in Acts 2:41-47, a Greek methodology of writing that indicates the main point of the writing: "the centre is always the turning point."[2] The chiastic structure in Acts 2 has two repeated themes that point to the center of the center, the emphasized point of the passage.[3] The outer most layers, Acts 2:41 and 2:47, share the repeated theme of numerical growth. The next inner layers, Acts 2:42-43 and 2:46-47, share the repeated theme of a witnessed communal life. At the center of the center lies Acts 2:44-45, the author's main point—in other words, what was responsible for numerical growth and a witnessed communal life (see fig. 3.1).

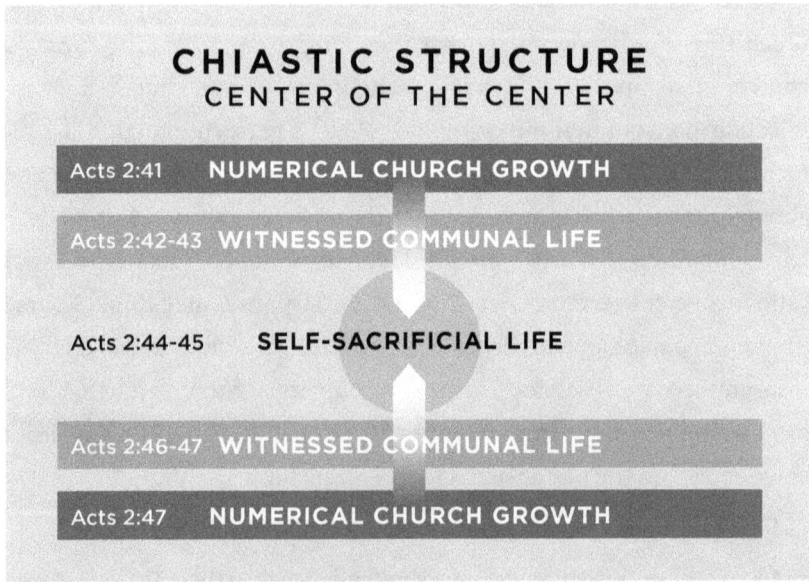

CHIASTIC STRUCTURE
CENTER OF THE CENTER

Acts 2:41	**NUMERICAL CHURCH GROWTH**
Acts 2:42-43	**WITNESSED COMMUNAL LIFE**
Acts 2:44-45	**SELF-SACRIFICIAL LIFE**
Acts 2:46-47	**WITNESSED COMMUNAL LIFE**
Acts 2:47	**NUMERICAL CHURCH GROWTH**

Figure 3.1. Chiastic structure of Acts 2

Luke's main point in describing the early church in this manner was that numerical church growth resulted from the self-sacrificial life of the early church. "All the believers were together and had everything in common. They sold property and possessions to give to anyone who had need" (Acts 2:44-45). Soong-Chan Rah asks, "So instead of seeing evangelism and church growth as the effect of the cause of a verbal proclamation and the preaching of the gospel by Peter, should we instead see evangelism and church growth as a product of the demonstration of the gospel in the self-sacrificial living of the church?"[4]

It would serve us well, both leaders and congregation, to reexamine what we put at the center of the center. Our expectation for fruitfulness should be connected to our faithfulness in how we live out self-giving love with one another and those in our city, community, and neighborhood. Instead of putting a requirement on pastors to be the most insightful orators who aspire to an unattainable metric of attendance growth, we should instead seek leaders who will help the congregation focus on the center of the center—who will model self-giving love in the ways of Jesus. Church growth then results not from sermons but through the church's demonstration of self-sacrificial communal life.

The congregation's second impossible pressure on the church leader is that of establishing an ideal community. While the sense of belonging is a deeply foundational piece of communal life in the church, we must be aware that our Western twenty-first-century interpretation of belonging is littered with individualism, materialism, and racism. Our desire for belonging is an individualistic one. Our desire for spiritual growth is a personal consumeristic one. And our desire for community is a homogeneous one, wishing to maintain a community made up of people like us (see table 3.1). In *The Great Reversal*, David Moberg notes that the lopsided emphasis on evangelism and omission of most aspects of social involvement have established the Western value of individualism and consumerism over the value of tending to communal needs.[5] Christine Pohl writes in her critical work *Living into Community*,

> Our yearnings to belong and our desire for lasting relationships, however, are often accompanied by uncertainty about making commitments. As one person put it, it would be so much easier if we could be "connected without being encumbered." Despite the fact that many of us claim to be dissatisfied with individualism, we cherish our capacity to make individual choices and to seek opportunities for personal growth. . . . While we might want community, it is often community on our terms, with easy entrances and exits, lots of choice and support, and minimal responsibilities. Mixed together, this is not a promising recipe for strong or lasting communities.[6]

Table 3.1. Mature versus immature leadership focus

Leadership expectation	Immature leadership focus	Mature leadership focus
Church growth	Sermon (without change)	Self-sacrificial life of the church
Ideal community	Social availability (without challenge)	Deep communal life of the church

The unattainable expectation placed on church leaders by the congregation to provide and sustain an ideal community that ultimately serves and meets the individual's personal, consumeristic, and homogeneous needs is also ultimately devoid of the characteristics that make up a Jesus community. A deep communal life moves away from an individualistic, materialistic, and racist focus and is transformed by Christ to radically love and serve one another and the surrounding community in a self-giving way that makes the world turn to Jesus.

MATURE LEADERS ARE DISCIPLES FIRST

Even with renewed clarity regarding the communal self-sacrificial focus required of mature church leaders and their congregations, and away from impossible power pressures on the pastor, an approach to change may not be clear. We are in desperate need of maturity markers of leadership in the church. Maturity markers do several things: they help to determine what we value, anticipate progression, and identify who to emulate. They also provide a process for examining the tension of personal felt needs and idealized expectations.

In defining the maturity markers of church leadership, I expect that leaders, as imitators of Jesus, should be pursuing discipleship. Mature leaders are disciples first. Imitator of Jesus, not leader, is the core of their identity. Therefore, the maturing leader is engaging in Christlike character, Christlike theology, Christlike wisdom, and Christlike missional living.[7] Every disciple is maturing in both spiritual confidence (identity) and social competence (praxis) within a community on mission together for the sake of their city, community, and neighborhood. If the leader is not a disciple of Jesus, then the leader has chosen someone or something else as a pattern. Our praxis is determined by our identity and vice versa; only a Christlike leader can lead a congregation to be Christlike. If Christianity without discipleship is Christianity without Christ,[8] then Christian leadership without discipleship is also leadership without Christ. Henri Nouwen offers this:

> Our vocation as Christians is to follow Jesus on his downward path and to become witnesses to God's compassion in the concrete situation of our time and place. Our temptation is to let needs for success, visibility, and influence dominate our thoughts, words, and actions to such an extent that we are gripped in the destructive spiral of upward mobility and thus lose our vocation. It is this lifelong tension between vocation and temptation that presents us with the necessity of spiritual formation.[9]

He continues regarding discipleship, "Formation is transformation, and transformation means a growing conformity to the mind of Christ, who did not cling to his equality with God but emptied himself. Thus discipleship cannot be realized without discipline."[10]

When the leader is a disciple first, then daily practice of living like Jesus naturally spills over into leading like Jesus. As a disciple already contends with the powers and principalities of this world (Rom 8:38-39), the leader is poised to contend against the underlying negative desires. The disciple who is already living a missional lifestyle becomes a leader who teaches the congregation to value the larger community. And finally, the leader who is imitating Jesus invites the congregation to have closer proximity to Jesus, not to himself or herself. On the other hand, when leaders are not disciples first, their character, thought, decision-making, and lifestyle are being formed by something or someone else. Then they will be pressured by church growth and ideal community, perpetually moving the church inward and orienting the congregation around themselves (see fig. 3.2).

Discipleship is crucial to Christian leaders. Its centrality allows them to lead the church to center discipleship, which connects the congregation to the community it exists in and for. Discipleship anchors the leader to imitate Jesus' way of doing leadership. Discipleship also sheds light on how the leader contends with power. And finally, maturing in Christlikeness allows the church to imitate Jesus and not desire proximity just to the leader.

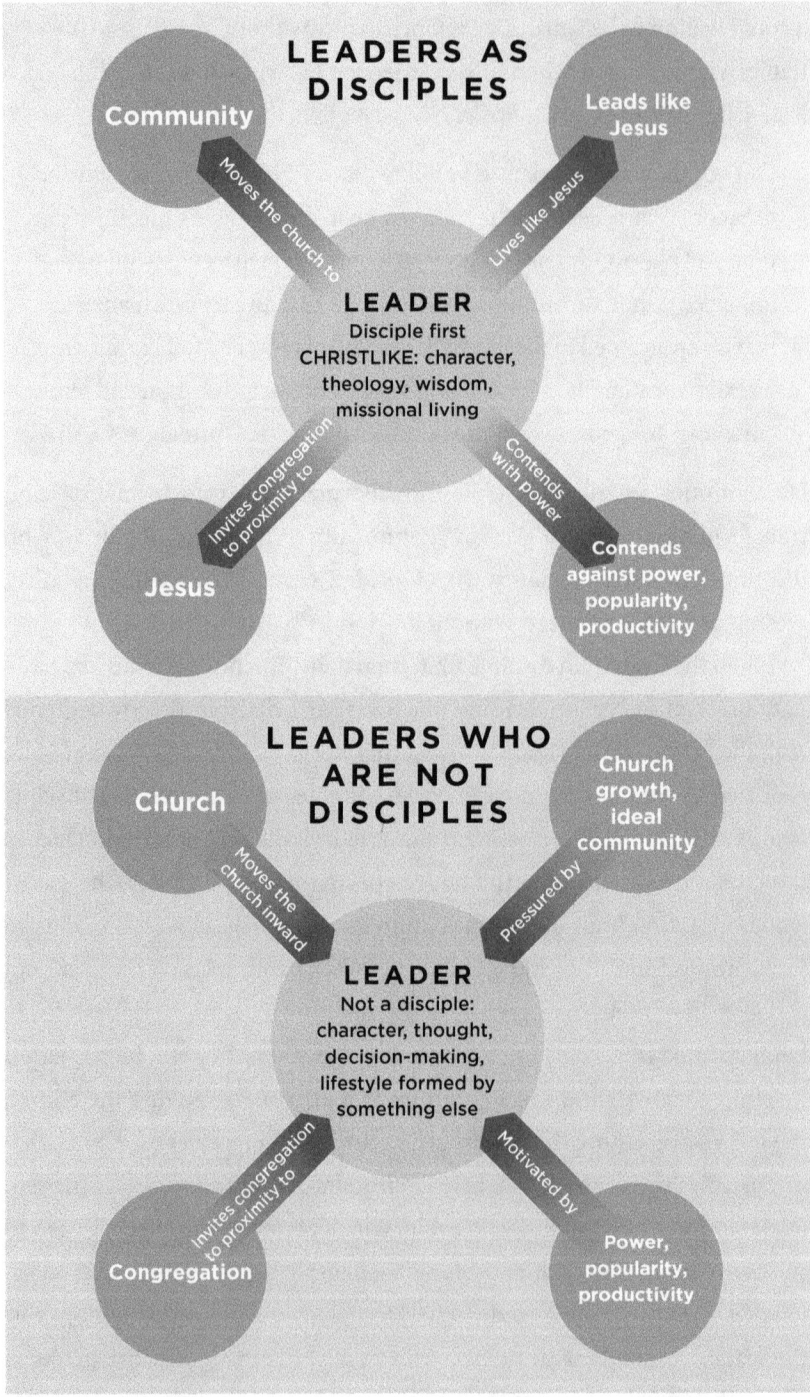

LEADERS AS DISCIPLES

Community

Leads like Jesus

Moves the church to

Lives like Jesus

LEADER
Disciple first
CHRISTLIKE: character,
theology, wisdom,
missional living

Invites congregation
to proximity to

Contends
with power

Jesus

Contends
against power,
popularity,
productivity

LEADERS WHO ARE NOT DISCIPLES

Church

Church
growth,
ideal
community

Moves the
church inward

Pressured by

LEADER
Not a disciple:
character, thought,
decision-making,
lifestyle formed by
something else

Invites congregation
to proximity to

Motivated by

Congregation

Power,
popularity,
productivity

Figure 3.2. Leaders as disciples versus leaders who are not disciples

MARKS OF MATURITY IN LEADERSHIP

So what do mature *leaders* look like? What are their motivations for leadership? And what is their impact on the community?

Mature leaders who are imitating Jesus gain rights to decision-making because they actively give up control. They are the most influential because they intentionally include and elevate others while de-centering themselves. Consequently, they earn deep respect in the community because of the growth of their inner life, which is expressed in their outward living.

The best way to know if there are mature leaders in the church is to see the impact on the church and the larger community. Who are the people who intentionally empower others and invite them to join in decision-making? Who are the people who celebrate others and connect them in relationship with one another? Who are the people whom the community respects and imitates because they remind the people of Christ?

In my local church, Meli is a mature leader. It wasn't because she graduated from one of the most selective law schools in the country nor because she clerked for Hawaii's Supreme Court. Nor is it because she is a senior staff attorney at one of the most respected nonprofit law firms in the state. Meli is a mature leader in our community because in the room, in any room, she empowers others, celebrating them, connecting them to one another, and she is the first to remind others of Jesus. Despite her petite frame (she's about 5'2" and barely 100 lb.), Meli has a gravitas, a weight of spiritual mass about her. Craig Barnes says about this gravitas,

> The old seminary professors used to speak about a necessary trait for pastoral ministry called gravitas. It refers to a soul that has developed enough spiritual mass to be attractive, like gravity. It makes the soul appear old, but gravitas has nothing to do with age. It has everything to do with wounds that have healed well, failures that have been redeemed, sins that have been forgiven, and thorns that have settled into the flesh. These severe experiences with life expand the soul until it appears larger than the body that contains it. Then it is large

enough to proclaim a holy joy, which is what makes the pastor's soul so attractive.[11]

If you encounter Meli, you might not notice her. She's quiet and demure, never seeking attention. The second of three children and only daughter to a Filipino American father and a Japanese American mother, many generations in Oahu, she's friendly but not overtly. She's intelligent but never comes off as pretentious. She can easily attract a crowd because people enjoy being with her. She's thoughtful but not calculating. Her personality is also warm and steady, and she is physically attractive. (My first-generation Korean mother refers to Meli as the "pretty one.") Meli could so easily wield control, crowd, and contribution to her own advantage. She is often the cleverest person in the room and could acquire control without batting an eye. (Trust me; I've seen her at work in one of those break-out rooms, and with the pressure of having to escape in less than sixty minutes, her small frame becomes commanding.) Meli is also almost always the most educated and accomplished person in the room; she could have had her pick in pursuing a career in corporate or government law. And who wouldn't want to be led by a smart, attractive, and accomplished person?

Meli demonstrates that she is a mature leader because she never assumes authority over others despite her ability. Time and time again, when invited into leadership spaces and conversations, she often asks, Whose voices are we missing at the table in order to make the best decision? Though she could easily draw a crowd around her, she makes sure that the community puts their gaze not on her but on Jesus and on one another. When others look to her because of her achievements and abilities, she is the first to genuinely celebrate and esteem those around her. Meli is a mature leader because she wields her ability so that the community is more empowered and celebrated and has a relatable model for Christlikeness.

When I first brought up the thought of leadership years ago with Meli, she laughed nervously and rolled her eyes, "Don't be ridiculous! I'm not a leader; I can't lead!" Then, as she grew more and more in her own discipleship, falling in love with discipling and equipping others, and discovering how much her heart ached for the church, she disqualified herself because of her anxiousness. "Maybe I shouldn't lead because I struggle with anxiety from time to time, and I'll never know when it'll show up." She would minimize it and often laugh it off, but in her innermost, deepest part, Meli wrestled profoundly with anxiety—for decades. She tearfully told me stories of so many instances of it spiraling out of control and leaving her mentally, emotionally, and even physically paralyzed. She shared how she tried so hard to keep it contained, but it would inevitably spill over into relationships, leaving a trail of hurt and harsh words she wished she could immediately retract.

Meli exhibits her mature leadership to all the community, a result of her insanely deep-rooted and hard-won connection with Jesus. No one in our church would guess that she struggles with anxiety since she is so poised and keeps her anxiety contained. We all know Meli for her gentleness, wide-openness, and assuredness toward herself and others. Anxiety is prevalent in our community, and perpetually more accentuated post-pandemic, but Meli is the most calming presence in the room. When the devastating fires hit Lahaina, Maui, in August 2023, our church connected quickly with the community to support families who had lost loved ones and generational homes to the torrential flames, one of the deadliest US wildfires in more than a century.[12] In addition to meeting financial, food, and supplies needs, we hosted a public service for the community.

When Meli invited a room packed with over a hundred people, both Jesus followers and non–Jesus followers, to lament together, equipping the community to address a God who laments with us, there was a profoundly deep sense of calm. Where anxiety should have been roaring its ugly head, it was replaced by calm, as Meli, softly wiping tears from her own eyes, spoke and prayed on behalf of a people who experienced such loss. How?

Over the years, as Meli grew more as a disciple of Jesus, she started inviting Jesus to sit with her daily in her innermost part, the part she felt was the ugliest and most destructive to others, the part that should disqualify her from leadership. Meli gave up control to Jesus. And Jesus began to prune. And this kind of deep pruning through discipleship is what produces in Meli even more fruitfulness. Meli's leadership is even more fruitful because she is a disciple first; she invites Jesus each day to form her character, thoughts, decision-making, and lifestyle; and she says yes to seasons of deep pruning.

THE FOUR Hs

4

*The awareness of the ambiguity of one's highest achievements (as
well as one's deepest failures) is a definite symptom of maturity.*

ROBERT LOUIS STEVENSON

*Then we will no longer be infants, tossed back and forth by the
waves, and blown here and there by every wind of teaching and
by the cunning and craftiness of people in their deceitful scheming.
Instead, speaking the truth in love, we will grow to become in every
respect the mature body of him who is the head, that is, Christ.*

EPHESIANS 4:14-15

AMERICAN COMEDIAN AND WRITER HASAN MINHAJ tells a joke
about how it seems that everyone is going to therapy. And people have
chosen to talk about it in newfound fancy terms like it's some sort of badge
of honor. He admits that there's nothing wrong with going to therapy and
unpacking trauma (especially the mental health issues exposed by the pandemic), but he's annoyed by society bragging about it. He quips, "Therapy
has to be like a haircut. You can't tell us about it. We have to notice
the difference."[1]

Obviously, comedy is a satirical and exaggerated medium, but Minhaj does have a point: the best way to show that you're working through something is for others to notice it. There should be some sort of mark indicating a change or growth. It's much the same in church leadership. There should be marks of mature leadership the leader doesn't have to tell us about. We should notice the difference.

When we consider possible marks of leadership, most churches utilize Paul's recommendations for choosing overseers and servants in 1 Timothy 3:1-13 and Titus 1:5-9. He directs elders and deacons to be faithful in marriage, rear obedient children, and be temperate in their use of alcohol, anger, arguments, and assets—essentially be upstanding citizens. To the Jesus communities in Thessalonica, Paul references the leaders by telling the church to "respect those who labor among you and are over you in the Lord and admonish you, and . . . esteem them very highly in love because of their work" (1 Thess 5:12-13 ESV).

We can see that these descriptions of roles of overseers (*episkopos*) in the churches in Ephesus and Crete, led by Timothy and Titus, respectively, are intended to guide the selection of leaders among a growing church community. Though both Timothy and his mentor Paul were never married and were childless, these descriptions were intended to pertain to the cultural context of the two regions addressed. We should not assume that only married men with children can lead, particularly when Paul includes women in other contexts. Professor Nijay Gupta adds:

> No named person is called an *episkopos*, so we cannot name a female overseer, nor a male one for that matter. Now, one *could* make the case that only men served as *episkopoi* because of the instructions in 1 Timothy 3:1-7. In that passage, Paul instructs that overseers must be the "husband of one wife" (1 Tim 3:2 NET) and must manage household and children well (1 Tim 3:4). A couple of things should be said about this. First, household management was a shared duty that husband and wife carried out together in Greco-Roman homes, so by itself that doesn't restrict the role to men (see 1 Tim 5:14).

Second, the emphasis on "one wife" is less about men leading (to the exclusion of women) and more about fidelity in marriage. But it is worth addressing the fact that this passage does default to the assumption of a male overseer. There is a simple reason for this—men would have naturally comprised the majority of leaders. . . . If Paul wanted to forbid women from aspiring to those roles, he could have. But as it stands, I take it that only a small number of Christian women were in a position to carry out that role.[2]

Contrast these descriptions to how Paul describes leaders in Thessalonica— those who labor with you, lead you, and correct you—devoid of lifestyle descriptors. Furthermore, there are many accounts of women also leading with Paul during his ministries.[3] It would be remiss of us to assume that the instructions for Ephesus and Crete were a generalized prescription for all churches. Paul most likely spoke to these contexts specifically.

Perhaps a better place to see what biblical leadership looks like can be found in the Gospel accounts.

A dispute also arose among them [the disciples] as to which of them was considered to be greatest. Jesus said to them, "The kings of the Gentiles lord it over them; and those who exercise authority over them call themselves Benefactors. But you are not to be like that. Instead, the greatest among you should be like the youngest, and the one who rules like the one who serves. For who is greater, the one who is at the table or the one who serves? Is it not the one who is at the table? But I am among you as one who serves." (Luke 22:24-27)

Also,

When [Jesus] had finished washing [the disciples'] feet, he put on his clothes and returned to his place. "Do you understand what I have done for you?" he asked them. "You call me 'Teacher' and 'Lord,' and rightly so, for that is what I am. Now that I, your Lord and Teacher, have washed your feet, you also should wash one another's feet. I have set you an example that you should do as I have done for you.

Very truly I tell you, no servant is greater than his master, nor is a messenger greater than the one who sent him. Now that you know these things, you will be blessed if you do them." (John 13:12-17)

A key point in biblical leadership is the motivation behind leading. Do we lead because of position, advantage, or gain? Can we lead out of low position, disadvantage, and loss? Jesus' remarks about leadership always revolved around service and the need to lead sacrificially. The Greek word *diakoneō* translated as "serves" in Luke 22:27 also means "minister to" or "tend to." Each of these words connotes proximity, personal interaction, coming to the same level in order to lean toward, and a deep sense of presence with others. Jesus' example of washing the disciples' feet and telling them to do likewise showed them that the motivation behind leadership is service. In this case, incarnational, self-giving love. Leadership is not an invitation to exploit, manipulate, or take by force; to Jesus, the motivation for leadership is an invitation for self-giving love. When our motivation for leading is power, popularity, or productivity, the community becomes disempowered, dependent, and deprived (see table 4.1).

Table 4.1. How underlying desires impact the community

Leadership trait	Type of authority	Underlying desire	Impact on community
Control	Decision making (competence)	Power	Disempowered
Crowd	Relational (influence)	Popularity	Dependent
Contribution	Accomplishment (experience)	Productivity	Deprived

As Jesus followers, our personal maturity is judged by our ability to follow his example of self-giving love in the church and larger community. As we as disciples imitate Jesus, so we as leaders imitate Jesus' leadership. This is the maturation process that Jesus exemplifies—growth through self-giving love: *teleiōtēs* through *kenōsis*.[4]

A person growing through self-giving love that empowers others, celebrates others, and is a Christlike example for others demonstrates the marks of maturity for church leadership. The four marks of mature leadership I look for, that help me identify a leader who is growing through self-giving love, are humility, honor, hospitality, and hope. The four Hs. Mature leaders in the church are always the most humble, honoring, hospitable, and hopeful people in the room. Their discipleship (or imitation of Jesus) produces these characteristics, their calling to leadership recognizes them, and their congregation and community flourish through them. Mature leaders make decisions through the lens of the four Hs. They gather and mobilize others through and around the four Hs. And they garner weightiness because of their consistent participation in these marks.

These marks are less of a metric but a progression. Our study of the Bible reveals these four marks to be intertwined and developing in a specific procession. If a mark of maturity is developed in a leader out of order, it is often short-lived. The progression starts with humility. Maturity in humility produces honor in the leader. Maturity in honor produces hospitality. Maturity in hospitality produces hope. As the leader's maturity starts with humility and progresses to hope, the entire community flourishes with the gift that comes from establishing a culture of humility, honor, hospitality, and hope—much more than it would with a leadership that desires power, popularity, and productivity. This is how leaders mature through self-giving love.

We will examine each marker: how each one deepens as the maturity journey progresses, how they are bound together in maturity, and what contends against each stage. We will close with how mature leaders require sharing leadership.

WHY HUMILITY, HONOR, HOSPITALITY, AND HOPE

When our motivation for leading comes out of humility, honor, hospitality, and hope, the community is invited into decision-making, relationship with one another, and actively imitating those who are actively imitating Christ. When these four Hs are the motivation for our leadership, we readily and wisely give up control because we trust that God is in control.

Table 4.2. How mature marks of leadership impact the community

Leadership trait	Type of authority	Mature motivation, the four Hs	Leadership action	Leadership why	Impact on community
Control	Decision-making (competence)	Humility, honor, hospitality, hope	Readily and wisely gives up control	Trusts deeply that God is in control	Empowers the community and invites them in decision making
Crowd	Relational (influence)	Humility, honor, hospitality, hope	De-centers themselves	Treats others as God's image bearers	Celebrates the community and invites them into relationship with one another
Contribution	Accomplishment (experience)	Humility, honor, hospitality, hope	Actively works on inner life that contributes to outward living	Understands God's value that everything we do flows from the heart	Respects and models after those who are imitating Jesus

We de-center ourselves because we treat others as fellow image bearers. We actively pay attention to our inner life, which contributes to our outward living because we understand God's intention that everything we do should flow from our heart. Our leadership ability to have control comes from trust, to mobilize the crowd comes from centering others, and to make contributions comes from our inner life with Christ.

Let's see how each of the four Hs works as a leadership progression of growth through self-giving love.

HUMILITY

Maya Angelou in an interview said,

> You see, I have no patience with modesty. Modesty is a learned adaptation. . . . You don't want modesty, you want humility. Humility comes from inside out. It says someone was here before me and I'm here because I've been paid for. I have something to do and I will do that because I'm paying for someone else who has yet to come.[5]

Humility is not modesty. Modesty is socialized through gender, race, and class in our culture whereas humility is universal among gender, race, and class. Modesty in gender, not humility, is speaking when women are praised for deflecting or dismissing praise and accomplishments and portrayed as narcissistic when embracing compliments. Modesty in race, not humility, is speaking when BIPOC leaders allow White leaders to take credit for their contributions but are portrayed as unwilling to be collaborative when embracing credit for their own accomplishments. Modesty in class, not humility, is speaking when socioeconomically elevated persons can climb a social and economic ladder by deliberately undermining their own competence because of their assurance that their power and position are not at risk. Not everyone can afford the social or economic consequences of minimizing themselves.

It seems that our culture understands humility to mean not minimizing our abilities, appreciating our own circumstances and accomplishments while equally appreciating those of others, and having a posture of empathy toward and listening to others. A humble and diminutive person is usually likable at best or in the least, not a threat. But what does God have to say about humility?

When Jesus reveals himself to his disciples, he says in Matthew,

> All things have been committed to me by my Father. No one knows the Son except the Father, and no one knows the Father except the Son and those to whom the Son chooses to reveal him.
>
> Come to me, all you who are weary and burdened, and I will give you rest. Take my yoke upon you and learn from me, for I am gentle and humble in heart, and you will find rest for your souls. For my yoke is easy and my burden is light. (Mt 11:27-30)

In this passage, Jesus reveals his true identity and thus his manner of leading. His identity is deeply connected to the Father, and his work is deeply connected to rest. He's talking about both his identity and purpose. From this example we learn of Jesus' gentleness and humility in heart.

Humility is about knowing and operating from our true self. And when we find our true self through our deep connection with God and our work that is rooted in rest, we begin to value what Jesus values and lead the way Jesus leads.

There is much to learn about Jesus' humility in Philippians 2:1-11, which presents a healthy starting point for leaders.

> Therefore if you have any encouragement from being united with Christ, if any comfort from his love, if any common sharing in the Spirit, if any tenderness and compassion, then make my joy complete by being like-minded, having the same love, being one in spirit and of one mind. Do nothing out of selfish ambition or vain conceit. Rather, in humility value others above yourselves, not looking to your own interests but each of you to the interests of the others.
>
> In your relationships with one another, have the same mindset as Christ Jesus:
>
> Who, being in very nature God,
>> did not consider equality with God something to be used to
>>> his own advantage;
>
> rather, he made himself nothing
>> by taking the very nature of a servant,
>> being made in human likeness.
>
> And being found in appearance as a man,
>> he humbled himself
>> by becoming obedient to death—
>> even death on a cross!
>
> Therefore God exalted him to the highest place
>> and gave him the name that is above every name,
>
> that at the name of Jesus every knee should bow,
>> in heaven and on earth and under the earth,
>
> and every tongue acknowledge that Jesus Christ is Lord,
>> to the glory of God the Father.

Jesus' humility, which anchors his identity to a relationship to God and his work to resting in God, is what prevents him from acting to his own advantage and causes him to value others above himself and look to the interests of others. Because of Jesus' humility, he does nothing out of selfish ambition or vain conceit. He was exalted to the highest place because his humility was an act of self-emptying, *kenōsis*.

Humility requires self-emptying, which enables us to value others and their interests above ourselves because it allows us to see ourselves less. And the repetitive act of self-emptying, humility, can only be done when the self-emptying roots us deeper in our identity (relationship deeply connected to God) and our purpose (work deeply connected to rest). Without that rootedness, the leader will instead turn to the opposite of *kenōsis*, *harpagmos*. This Greek word, while tame in our English translation, is synonymous with using to one's advantage, grasping on to something, seizing by force, robbing from someone, raping someone, and taking for oneself.[6] The opposite of self-emptying is looking at something or someone that is good in your own eyes and taking it for yourself.

When Adam and Eve were deceived by the serpent and ate from the tree of the knowledge of good and evil, *harpagmos* was present: "When the woman saw that the fruit of the tree was good for food and pleasing to the eye, and also desirable for gaining wisdom, she took some and ate it. She also gave some to her husband, who was with her, and he ate it" (Gen 3:6). When King David saw Bathsheba bathing and took Uriah's wife for himself (2 Sam 11:2-4), *harpagmos* was present.

Jesus' humility is what inspires a leader to practice *kenōsis* versus *harpagmos*: to lead with self-emptying and self-giving love versus leading by taking something for our own advantage, selfish ambition, or vain conceit. James contributes further,

> Who is wise and understanding among you? Let them show it by their good life, by deeds done in the humility that comes from wisdom. But if you harbor bitter envy and selfish ambition in your hearts, . . . there you find disorder and every evil practice. (Jas 3:13-14, 16)

From the very beginning, there have been two kinds of wisdom—what God sees as good and gives to us and what we see as good and take for ourselves. Humility anchors the leader to the truth that God intends good for us and our community and reassures us that we need not take for ourselves. Humility helps us to reject the serpent's lie that God does not intend good for us or our community and withholds from us. Humility allows us to give up control to God because of our deep relationship with God and rest. Humility allows leaders to trust God, give up control, de-center themselves, and contribute to what God is already doing in the world.

The strange and beautiful thing about humility and the practice of self-emptying is that the telos is not what you would imagine. God lifts up the humble; he exalts those who actively give themselves over to love others. Jesus' act of humility, emptying himself for the sake of others, is the reason he is exalted to the highest place. God honors the humble (Jas 4:10). A leader who does not mature in humility will not progress to the next stage in maturity, which is honor.

HONOR

In our Western culture, the word *honor* feels like an archaic word reserved for military members and dignitaries for their services or offices, or for funerals when we are paying our respects for a loss. It seems that in cultural norms related to honor, we are really referring to the word *honorable*. Being honorable has the sense of morality mixed with decorum. A person is seen as honorable because he or she chose to do the "right thing" or attained a certain level of status. Those regarded with great respect in our culture are usually those with positions of power. Society pays greater regard to those who are positioned above others, whether socially, economically, or academically. In addition, in most honor-shame based cultures, including the Asian and Mediterranean diaspora, the term *honor* is associated with actively avoiding collective or communal shame.[7]

It seems when God addresses honor, it's akin to this insight from Marilynne Robinson: "At the root of real honor is always the sense of the sacredness of the person who is its object."[8] Describing the historical culture from the biblical Mediterranean era, J. K. Campbell adds, "Honor is always a question of ascription, not a matter of fact or individual right."[9]

The Hebrew word *kabod* in Proverbs 15:33 is translated as "honor": "Wisdom's instruction is to fear the Lord, / and humility comes before honor." However, כָּבוֹד can also be translated as "glory," "abundance," "splendor," "reputation," and "dignity."[10] The verb form for honor, *kabad*, can be translated "to honor," "to give weight to," "to promote," and "to make heavy."[11] The verb translated "honor" in the command to "honor your father and your mother" in Exodus 20:12 is the same verb used to describe Yahweh bringing glory to himself in Exodus 14:4. Honor has a lot to do with placing weight and substance on something or someone—a way to value or measure worth.

My own family has experienced culturally determined measures of honor. My Korean American immigrant family did what Korean immigrant families do—we take our children to see Korean pediatricians. My dad took me to Dr. Choi in North Philadelphia for my school-mandated annual exams. We always went late at night to his sterile pale-green office, since my parents worked seven days a week and for long hours. Both Dr. Choi and my dad were men of very few words. I remember vividly that Dr. Choi never made eye contact with my dad. Except for one time.

When I was eighteen, I went with my dad to get my college health forms filled out. Very routine. Dr. Choi didn't skip a beat and did the exam without once making eye contact with my dad—until he asked what college I was attending in the fall. My dad, usually sitting very stoically and submissively in that pale-green chair in the exam room, sat a little taller. This was the moment he was waiting for. "The University of Pennsylvania," he said, a little louder than his usual monotone.

Dr. Choi stopped. He turned and faced my dad. Dr. Choi looked at my dad! "Oh, congratulations!"

My pediatrician had no regard for my low-class father until he found out I was admitted to an Ivy League institution. However, because Dr. Choi placed a great deal of weight on academic achievement and socioeconomic status, this one time he was moved to acknowledge my father. What we place value on, what we give weight to, informs how and whom we honor.

Paul exhorts in Romans 12:10, "Be devoted to one another in love. Honor one another above yourselves." The practice of honoring others is key to leaders because it shapes how they see others. Whom do leaders bestow honor on? Whom do they highlight in the community? Is it people with ability? Resources? Good looks? Connections?

While sharing with me a bit about their church in one of the most diverse and lowest socioeconomic neighborhoods in London, Ben and Sarah stopped and looked at each other. Their eyes were filled with tears. They had experienced so much pain and misunderstanding in their own leadership over the years, but their tears weren't for themselves. They had remembered how some folks from the neighborhood, who had never been a part of a church community before, were finding a home with them.

Ben and Sarah loved these people, shared about each one by name, their backstory, their struggles, and most importantly, how they loved to worship God. However, each of them had a very prominent physical and neural disability. While many in their church felt like they were distractions, Ben and Sarah wanted to honor them; they even had these new participants lead the community in worship. Ben was the leader who first told me that discipleship can be defined as imitating Jesus in both "spiritual confidence and social competence."[12] He was leading his congregation not just in growing in spiritual confidence, their Christlike identity, but more importantly, in social competence, their Christlike praxis. Ben was leading his church to honor God by honoring others.

In their seminal book *Disabling Leadership*, Andrew T. Draper, Jody Michele, and Andrea Mae implore,

> People with disabilities leading in the church is a matter of experiencing the whole body of Christ. It is not a matter of including a few folks with disabilities as tokens. We are taking the radical step of claiming, with the apostle Paul, that if all the body parts are not present and honored, then the body of Christ is not present

(1 Corinthians 12:14-25). The church is the one group in society that is necessarily constituted by the diversity of its members, especially those deemed by society as weaker, less productive, or more disposable. More than any other community, the church is recognized by the ways people who are marginalized, especially people with disabilities, are included and honored in her midst.[13]

I look for leaders who honor others, delight in celebrating others, because it shows me that they see all of humanity as image bearers of God in the world. It's not a coincidence that the word *kabod* is used most often to describe the character of God, his glory, splendor, and fullness of weight. And it's no coincidence that God created humanity in his image to be full of glory, splendor, and fullness of weight.

While humility helps us as leaders to see ourselves less, it's honor that helps us to see *more* in others. Since we are all made in the image of God, we all are given highest regard. As leaders, we can freely esteem, highlight, and celebrate others—celebrate what God is doing in them, through them, and around them. In many ways, the practice of honoring others is the practice of honoring God.

The most practical way to cultivate the practice of honor is to practice celebrating others. Celebrating helps to counter honor's *harpagmos*, envy. Envy is often listed in Scripture with other sins that destroy fellowship. Christine Pohl, in her extensive work on Christian communal practices shares,

> Envy generates and reproduces misery because it is accompanied by distrust, malice, and uncertainty. When we are envious, it shows in backbiting, grumbling, and resentment. We tend to disparage and minimize the accomplishments of others, or to challenge the standards by which accomplishments are measured.[14]

In my local congregation, as in so many faith communities, our biggest sin issue is envy. I sincerely hate it. There have been many times I thought our community wasn't going to survive because of envy. Envy fractures relationships and undermines communal work. It's insidious and often so hidden that it comes out as mere comparison, struggles with self-disqualification, allegations of an unfair system, suspicions of being left out, or accusations of boasting. Envy caused some of our most missional-minded leaders to hesitate because they didn't want to be blamed for other people's discontent or resentment.

Every year we participate in intentional practices of celebrating one another instead of resorting to envy. We're still not really great at it, but while it has been painful and difficult work, it has allowed me to experience the gift of maturity in those who are able to honor others. There's this beautiful quality of honoring others: maturity grows not from the person being honored wanting more honor but from the person who is honored giving it away to others. Leaders who honor others establish a community that delights in honoring one another. Honoring others also helps us to experience God's way of making space for others. If the leader does not mature in honor, he or she will not understand or progress to the next stage in maturity, which has everything to do with making space for others, hospitality.

HOSPITALITY

The hospitality industry spends $1.5 trillion on marketing each year and is based on a strategy taught in hospitality industry courses around "Product, Price, Promotion, and Place."[15]

> As these marketing fundamentals evolve to meet modern guest demands and digital-era challenges, hotel marketers [*churches*] are presented with an opportunity to redefine their strategies. Harnessing technology, data, and innovative tactics to create exceptional guest experiences and drive revenue [*church attendance*] is paramount in this ever-evolving landscape.[16]

In the statement above, I have suggested in italics substitutions that will sound pretty familiar to most of us who have gone to our fair share of pastoral conferences. Oftentimes, the product-based hospitality industry and the hospitality of the church seem interchangeable, as most of our strategies for increasing hospitality have to do with meeting the individualistic, comfort-craving demands of the modern church attendee.

Contrary to hospitality being a church-growth strategy, it flows from the leader who exhibits humility and practices honor; hospitality is the resulting mature mark of leadership. Rather than host an entertaining experience, a mature leader makes space and holds space for a diverse set of people to experience unity and not division. "Hospitality is at the heart of Christian life, drawing from God's grace and reflecting God's graciousness. In hospitality, we respond to the welcome that God has offered and replicate that welcome in the world."[17] Hospitality is what allows a community to endure over time.

Alexia Salvatierra and Brandon Wrencher write about the historical movement of base ecclesial churches in Latin America and the Philippines in the late twentieth century and the efforts among Brown and Black church communities to provide hospitality for those who were least welcomed in the antebellum era of the United States. "The paradox between creating a safe haven and the call to risky love and reconciliation is an important feature of both movements that provokes and inspires us today."[18] It extends beyond making space and holding space for enemies to become friends; it makes the unwelcomed most welcomed.

In contrast, the *harpagmos* of hospitality is actively creating spaces of division. Instead of making space and holding space for others, leaders without hospitality take up space. They are motivated by the desire to cache power or a fear of losing their power or status. They take up space to avoid personal cost or hoard personal gain. When power is used in this way, it decreases the congregation's ability to feel safe, seen, and sacred.

I remember taking an intercultural development inventory (IDI) class for church leaders and being the first to enter the room. I found a seat where I always like to sit, in the middle of the middle of the room. As the rest of my colleagues started pouring in, the room was immediately divided. There were two older White male pastors who were seated to my right; they had moved the classroom chairs so that they could spread their legs a bit more and be comfortable. One was leaning back relaxed. The other was looking at his watch for the session to start. To the left of me was a crowded group of participants, mostly Black, Brown, and women. The left side of the room felt lopsided with too many seats sardined together. While the right side of the room had loud conversation, the left side held whispered conversation. When our speaker, a young Afro-Latino Puerto Rican man came in, the left side of the room quieted down respectfully and the right side continued their conversation. In the course of the next sixty minutes of our time together, the right side interrupted the speaker, asked the majority of the questions, and had more speaking time than anyone else in the room, including the speaker.

I don't know if everyone can relate to this story, but I am sure that every BIPOC and woman church leader has experienced this scenario before. In the world where racial microaggressions[19] and effects of attributional am-biguity[20] are daily realities, the conscientious leader, who makes and holds space for others rather than taking up space at the expense of others, is pivotal.

Willie James Jennings believes radical hospitality is fundamental to the gospel:

> [In Acts] Paul is living under constrained conditions. . . . Yet Paul, in the midst of his constrained condition, enacts a future for himself in which he becomes a place. He decides to open up where he is—open his story, share his journey, announce the new thing that God is doing and wants to do in the world—to all who come to him. He will, with courage and conviction, open his life.
>
> What does it mean to become a place? I don't mean to have a place, but to *become* a place.
>
> It may seem odd to refer to a person as a place, but I am referring here to a kind of becoming through which one becomes a place of meeting, a place of gathering that opens up for people new possibilities of thriving life together even in, especially in, confined and confining spaces.

Jennings continues:

> We who name the name of Jesus are all faced with a decision that grows in urgency with each passing day, whether we will live in

places in ways that are inconsequential to the gospel we say guides our lives or whether we will root ourselves in a place and decide to become people whose very name becomes synonymous with a meeting and with a thriving together that others never thought possible. Such people who become a place will also become synonymous with another name that gathers together hopes and dreams rooted in a life that overcame death and promises an overcoming.[21]

The practice of hospitality, people becoming a place for others, becomes the doorway for leaders to cultivate a community of hope. Without the leader maturing in hospitality, he or she will not understand or progress to the next stage in maturity, hope.

HOPE

In her book *Caste*, Isabel Wilkerson writes regarding the unusual presidential election of former president Barack Obama in the wake of the 2008 housing crisis as the "greatest departure from the script of the American caste system."

Hope had been Obama's mantra during times that badly needed it. A record tide of people from the lower and middle castes, people who swelled with pride and whose votes now felt like a mission, came out for him, and, along with just enough dominant-caste voters who believed in him, too, swept Obama into the White House. The world was so joyous that a committee in Norway awarded him the Nobel Peace Prize within months of his inauguration. "Only very rarely has a person to the same extent as Obama captured the world's attention," the Nobel committee said, "and given its people hope for a better future."[22]

While hope can be categorized as desiring a brighter future, hope in our modern language often insinuates a fleeting sense, some flicker of distant light in the darkness and personal dreams being fulfilled. We can imagine a child with her fingers crossed, eyes closed, wishing for the pony she's always wanted. Wishful thinking.

Hope has been researched extensively in psychology and education; in fact, psychologist C. R. Snyder developed what is now called "hope theory," which many industries use, including school counselors, to help people attain their goals. Hope is defined as "a positive motivational state that is based on an interactively derived sense of successful (a) agency (goal-directed energy) and (b) pathways (planning to meet goals)."[23] Will power.

But biblical hope has much more to do with how we actively participate in what God is doing in us and in the world and acknowledging that God is doing it. Paul writes to the Jesus communities in Rome, "[W]e know that suffering produces perseverance; perseverance, character; and character, hope. And hope does not put us to shame, because God's love has been poured out into our hearts through the Holy Spirit, who has been given to us" (Rom 5:3-5). He continues in Romans 8,

> We know that the whole creation has been groaning as in the pains of childbirth right up to the present time. Not only so, but we ourselves, who have the firstfruits of the Spirit, groan inwardly as we wait eagerly for our adoption to sonship, the redemption of our bodies. For in this hope we were saved. But hope that is seen is no hope at all. Who hopes for what they already have? But if we hope for what we do not yet have, we wait for it patiently. (Rom 8:22-25)

Childbirth is so often a dramatic time of hope. I remember when each of my three kids was born. It's a wonder of human memories that the memories of our children's births continue to be so vivid. Beren was ten days late, natural birth with no epidural, at a birth center with midwives whom I loved, during an early morning storm. Steve and I laughed and cried so much. It was my shortest labor, having pushed for twenty minutes. We loved Beren the moment we met him.

Emma was way too early, an emergency C-section, premature birth, double nuchal cord. It was evening, and I demanded to sleep in the NICU with her. She was so fragile that Steve and I were nervous to change her diaper. We loved Emma the moment we met her.

Kyriella was right on time, a vaginal birth after the C-section. The obstetrician came running in just as I was pushing, exactly midday. Steve and I laughed and cried so much again. We loved Kyriella the moment we met her.

But each birth story doesn't begin with the day of birth; it starts nine months earlier. There's a longer story of love, commitment, and conflict resolutions. Steve and I faced reorienting our schedules, finances, and goals to prepare for each of them. And, of course, with each one there was physical pain and suffering, mental and emotional pain and suffering, and most of all, perseverance. We fully participated in the waiting and expectancy. We fully participated in hope.

Kelci, one of our local church's leaders, offers another example of maturity in hope. She is the director of Kaka'ako Kupuna, one of our missional communities, where she started years ago discipling a group of volunteers who were committed to serving a low-income senior living facility, Na Lei Hulu Kupuna (NLHK) in the neighborhood of Kaka'ako. It was a painful start. After almost a year of praying, discerning, and hesitating to live into this vision, she lost nearly twenty people when she first asked her community group if they wanted to join with her in serving the low-income seniors at NLHK. These are people she had shepherded and shared life with; only five agreed to go with her.

In the beginning, it was difficult to navigate how to "do ministry" without raising suspicion or diminishing dignity in this senior population, particularly because she is a young White female hospice-care nurse transplanted from Wisconsin. She stuck out like a sore thumb amid Asian and Polynesian octogenarians. After being disappointed by those who declined to assist, still other Christians challenged Kelci and her small team as they started hosting bingo and pizza nights at NLHK: How is this church? Where does Jesus come in? Who do you think you are?

When the global pandemic hit, Kelci's team changed from event planners to food-access coordinators. Throughout Covid-19, they worked tirelessly to provide one month's worth of groceries for every resident at NLHK, in addition to acquiring access to two other low-income senior living facilities in the same neighborhood. They made sure that all five hundred residents had food and hygiene supplies throughout the pandemic. And now post-pandemic, while the grandmas and grandpas continue to have access to basic needs, there are discipleship cores that have started in the buildings. There are seniors discipling one another as imitators of Jesus—seniors leading in their own apartment complexes to pray for their neighbors, share the gospel with them, and share resources. At NLHK, no resident is ever in need.

How did this happen? Kelci is a leader who has hope. I know this because she did not despair in the midst of pain; she persevered. She persevered when she was rejected by her people. She persevered when others questioned her. She persevered when the world was shutting down. She persevered when it seemed crazy for senior citizens to minister to one another. She persevered when it seemed impossible to multiply this flourishing work to two other residential facilities. Why did she persevere?

It may come as a surprise, but while Kelci's personality is kind and sweet, she doesn't come off as the "life of the party." She rarely demands attention, doesn't have quick comebacks, and would have been absolutely fine being the consummate "greeter" at church. But God gave her a vision that she just could not shake off. Hope is having a clarity about where you're headed. Kelci has a clarity that one day in Kakaʻako, because of Jesus, every low-income senior will feel seen and loved and valued; they will never experience loneliness, and they will fully participate in the community. Kelci has this vision because she is full of hope. Because of hope, she is able to persevere in the waiting while being fully expectant of what God is already doing in her neighborhood and promises to do.

Hope invites us to perseverance in lieu of despair.

Table 4.3. Marks of Maturity: Humility, Honor, Hospitality, Hope

Process of maturity	Means	Rival
Teleiōtēs	*Kenōsis*	*Harpagmos*
Growth	Self-giving love	Taking for oneself
Humility	Self-emptying	Selfish ambition
Honor	Celebrate others	Envying others
Hospitality	Making space	Taking up space
Hope	Perseverance	Despair

Lilly Shanahan and her research team write, "Despair, at the level of the individual, is a multifaceted construct with manifestations in different interrelated domains."[24] The interrelated domains include cognitive despair, emotional despair, behavioral despair, and biological despair. They continue, "The domains of despair are not limited to the individual; they can also permeate social contexts, including social networks and communities in which people are embedded."

Matthew Desmond and Adam Travis have observed,

> In the wake of such shared exposures, average levels of cognitive, emotional, behavioral, and biological despair may increase markedly in social groups and, in turn, further compound individual-level despair. Indeed, exposure to adversity in communities that are disadvantaged to begin with can lead to disengagement and declines in social cohesion, creating a pernicious cycle between the person and his or her community.[25]

Table 4.4. Multidisciplinary impact of despair[26]

Cognitive despair	Emotional despair	Behavioral despair	Biological despair
Defeat	Excessive sadness	High-risk behavior	Adrenal response
Hopelessness	Irritability	Addiction	Autonomic nervous system response
Guilt	Hostility	Abuse	Immune system
Worthlessness	Loneliness	Low physical activity	Obesity
Learned helplessness	Anhedonia	Self-harm	Hypertension
Pessimism	Apathy		Insomnia
Limited positive expectation for the future			Difficulty concentrating
			Pain

I want to echo research from psychology, sociology, and political science affirming that communal despair is not the fault of the community; it's the effect of what is happening to the community. For instance, when an urban Black and Brown neighborhood or an overtaken Indigenous tribe collectively exhibits biological despair after decades and generations of physical stressors, it should not be up to the community to repair this on their own. A sin has been done to these communities.

If a leader's approach does not include hope that comes from humility (a deep sense of who they are in Christ), honor (a deep sense of how they see others as fellow image bearers of God), and hospitality (a deep sense of making and holding space for others), then instead of persevering, they will move quickly to individualistic despair. Hope has a lot to do with how we respond to our current situations. Do we persevere or do we despair? Do we invite our community to persevere or to despair?

FOUR HS AND SHARING LEADERSHIP

The progression of the mature leader from humility to honor to hospitality and finally to hope results from *kenōsis* or self-giving love. This progression reminds the leader daily to resist *harpagmos*, taking power for oneself. It's what allows leaders to give up control to God, de-center themselves, and contribute to and invite the community into God's work in the world (see table 4.5).

Table 4.5. Process of maturity: four Hs

Means	*Teleiōtēs*: self-giving love, *kenōsis*	*Teleiōtēs*: taking for myself, *harpagmos*
Marks	Humility, honor, hospitality, hope	Selfish ambition, envy, division, despair
Practice	My identity is rooted in my relationship with God; my work is rooted in the rest I find in God.	My identity and work are dependent on my power, popularity, or productivity.
Motivation	Trust God and his goodness for me and for my community.	Don't trust God; I need to seize goodness for myself.
Result	Give up control to God, de-center myself, and contribute to God's work in the world.	Take control, center my leadership around a crowd, and increase my own contributions.

As leaders mature through *kenōsis*, they are also clarifying their relationship with God and their relationship with the community they are leading. Each step in the progression of maturing through the four Hs affects relationship with both God and community (see table 4.6).

Table 4.6. Effects of the four Hs on the leader's relationships with God and community

Marks of maturity	Leader's relationship with God	Leader's relationship with community
Humility	Trust God	With them
Honor	Esteem God	Celebrate them
Hospitality	Welcomed by God	Make space for them
Hope	Expectant	Give them vision

This kind of mature leadership is naturally tied to sharing leadership. The leaders who actively participate in the four Hs are the first leaders who share leadership; they expect to lead with others. Not only that, but leaders who are formed by the four Hs can sustain sharing leadership. While a solo leader often produces a disempowered, dependent, and deprived community, it takes a collaborative effort to empower the community and provide a full reflection of Christ through multiple models of those who are imitating Jesus: women and men, young and old, different ethnicities and race, laborer and professional. Those who show the four Hs in their leadership are poised for sharing leadership.

PART TWO

SHARING

LEADERSHIP IN

EPHESIANS 4

The church is called to embody the boundless love
of God by being a community of radical
welcome to all God's children.

ALEXIA SALVATIERRA

5

REVISING THE DELINEATION OF LEADERSHIP FROM EPHESIANS 4

It's time for the whole church, yes, the whole church, to take
a whole gospel on a whole mission to the whole world.

JOHN PERKINS

So Christ himself gave the apostles, the prophets, the evangelists, the
[shepherds] and teachers, to equip his people for works of service, so
that the body of Christ may be built up until we all reach unity
in the faith and in the knowledge of the Son of God and become
mature, attaining to the whole measure of the fullness of Christ.

EPHESIANS 4:11-13

I WAS INVITED TO TEACH a seminar on leadership for Black pastors in the DC metro area using the fivefold outline from Ephesians 4:11-13: Apostles, Prophets, Evangelists, Shepherds, and Teachers, more commonly known as APEST.[1] I could already sense the eyes either rolling or glazing over. These leaders were accomplished, led large Black or multicultural churches in one of the largest urban regions in the country, and ministered in an extremely fast-paced and intellectual world. I could imagine they had no interest in hearing about some obscure training on sharing leadership— and certainly not from a random Asian American church planter from Hawaii.

All the participants had read about APEST prior to the training, so I asked the group to divide into five groups as they identified with each APEST gifting and share why they identified with that gifting. Apostles here, Prophets there, Evangelists, then Shepherds over here, and, last but not least, Teachers in that corner. We collected words and descriptors that resonated far more culturally to these Black urban leaders than the designation they were provided. Then using these culturally resonating identifiers, we each shared about our own leadership journeys.

The room became more and more vulnerable as some shared how they felt they were misfits in church leadership and where their hearts truly came alive in community-development work or creative innovational work. Others admitted how exhausted they felt shepherding so many needy people. For most Black pastors, their people weren't just the church's members; these pastors also ministered to community members who claimed them as pastor. Still others felt they were identifying their calling for the first time after seeing alternatives beyond preaching and administration. In fact, they sensed God's call in what was happening outside the church. We spent five hours together that day, and when we finished, these Black pastors wanted more.

APEST AND LEADERS

In the contemporary Western church, there's a spectrum of opinion about APEST among pastors and leaders. At one end of the spectrum are those who see the fivefold framework of Apostle, Prophet, Evangelist, Shepherd, and Teacher as the God-given structure for serving within the church as well as living out our individual calling to God. Alan Hirsch writes about "5Q," his coined phrase to consider a quotient to measure a person's fivefold intelligence similarly to IQ and EQ scores measuring an individual's intellectual or emotional capacities, respectively.[2] He says, "The first clue to the divine origin of 5Q can be found in the first few chapters of Genesis. It has continued to intrigue us in that it enables us to gain insight into the archetypal aspects of what it means to be human, to be made in God's image, and to live in relation to God."[3]

On the other end of the spectrum are those who see the fivefold or APEST framework as an isolated observation in Scripture that is taken too far and leaves too many confused. Darryl Dash writes,

> APEST has become ubiquitous within the church planting and missional movement, but it's not without its critics. Ty Grigg argues that there's no evidence that the APEST schema was "a thing" in the early church before Constantine; that it's not clear what we mean when we define apostles, prophets, evangelists, shepherds, and teachers; and that the terms were meant to refer to those who led the church, not every believer. "We find a few schematic verses without their surrounding Scriptural context, without scholarly consultation, without a history of interpretation, and without seeing our own cultural biases."[4]

Taking into account that our perspectives land somewhere on this spectrum between APEST as having a divine origin and APEST as not biblically supported, I will use APEST as a way to discuss the importance not of the fivefold topology but of sharing leadership. In a contemporary world where leadership is often defined explicitly or implicitly through the lens of gender, age, privilege, access, temperament, or experience, it's helpful to further an existing conversation to help build both vocabulary and dialogue around actively sharing leadership.

Before diving into the Scripture that serves seemingly as a standalone on all things regarding APEST or fivefold topology (Eph 4:11-13), I'd like to revisit why this was important to first-century followers of Jesus and why it is still important to the twenty-first-century church. To begin our revisit, we'll look at the two more popularized Scripture passages that present "gifts" of the church and delineation of gifts, Romans 12:1-8 and 1 Corinthians 12:1-31. We will meditate on these passages through the lens of investigating the importance of sharing leadership.

UNITY IN ROMANS 12

In the epistle to the Romans, the apostle Paul is writing one of his later letters to the Jesus communities in Rome. There the church was culturally divided after the Roman emperor Claudius had previously exiled Jewish citizens from the city for five years. In Romans 1, Paul reminds the culturally divided church communities in Rome that the good news of Jesus means that both "Jews" (Jewish Christians) and "Gentiles" (non-Jewish Christians) are brought together as a new humanity and unified as the church. He continues in Romans 12:1-8:

> Therefore, I urge you, brothers and sisters, in view of God's mercy, to offer your bodies as a living sacrifice, holy and pleasing to God—this is your true and proper worship. Do not conform to the pattern of this world, but be transformed by the renewing of your mind. Then you will be able to test and approve what God's will is—his good, pleasing and perfect will.
>
> For by the grace given me I say to every one of you: Do not think of yourself more highly than you ought, but rather think of yourself with sober judgment, in accordance with the faith God has distributed to each of you. For just as each of us has one body with many members, and these members do not all have the same function, so in Christ we, though many, form one body, and each member belongs to all the others. We have different gifts, according to the grace given to each of us. If your gift is prophesying, then prophesy in accordance with your faith; if it is serving, then serve; if it is teaching, then teach; if it is to encourage, then give encouragement; if it is giving, then give generously; if it is to lead, do it diligently; if it is to show mercy, do it cheerfully.

While most readers begin this conversation about the diversity of the church with "for just as each of us has one body . . . ," we must remember that this was a whole letter, and Paul's intent regarding the diverse gifts of the church is set in the first paragraph of Romans 12. Paul implores the members of the Jesus communities in the city capital of the Roman Empire with words like "living sacrifice" and "proper worship." For first-century readers and listeners, words like *sacrifice* and *worship* would evoke their relationship to the temple. And any references to the temple would symbolically represent the presence of God or where God's presence dwells (See Ex 19:16-18; 40:34; 2 Chron 7:1; Ezek 4; Joel 3).

As Paul addresses a culturally divided region of churches, before he describes how diverse members can function as parts of one body, he implores the community to be collectively a dwelling place for God's presence. Most Western Christians read Romans 12:1 as a mandate for individual moral purity—that we are called individually and privately to commit our physical bodies to God, often in reference to sexual abstinence. But in truth Paul isn't talking about lifestyle practices; he's talking about what it means to be the church. We, with our differences and uniqueness, communally reflect God to the culture around us. We together make up the body; we not only belong to Christ, but "each member [also] belongs to all the others" (Rom 12:5).

The unity of the church, amid cultural differences, not only serves to ease tension; Paul also paints it as pivotal to reflecting God and experiencing the indwelling nature of God in the community. When we think of Paul's call for the unity of the church, we should also recognize that God's presence dwells in the unity of the diverse members of the church.

UNITY IN 1 CORINTHIANS 12

In the epistle to the Jesus communities in Corinth, the apostle Paul writes to one of the major cosmopolitan and economic port cities in the ancient world. He wants to address a few key issues in the Corinthians' church life, including divisiveness, sexual promiscuity, and food practices, and respond with the gospel of Jesus. When he gets to 1 Corinthians 12, he's addressing the chaotic public gatherings of the Corinthian churches—full of each person's preferences and members regularly interrupting one another, leaving observers and guests confused. He highlights the gospel response to contend against individual preferences with the theme of unity:

> There are different kinds of gifts, but the same Spirit distributes them. There are different kinds of service, but the same Lord. There are different kinds of working, but in all of them and in everyone it is the same God at work.

Now to each one the manifestation of the Spirit is given for the common good. To one there is given through the Spirit a message of wisdom, to another a message of knowledge by means of the same Spirit, to another faith by the same Spirit, to another gifts of healing by that one Spirit, to another miraculous powers, to another prophecy, to another distinguishing between spirits, to another speaking in different kinds of tongues, and to still another the interpretation of tongues. All these are the work of one and the same Spirit, and he distributes them to each one, just as he determines.

Just as a body, though one, has many parts, but all its many parts form one body, so it is with Christ. For we were all baptized by one Spirit so as to form one body—whether Jews or Gentiles, slave or free—and we were all given the one Spirit to drink. Even so the body is not made up of one part but of many.

Now if the foot should say, "Because I am not a hand, I do not belong to the body," it would not for that reason stop being part of the body. And if the ear should say, "Because I am not an eye, I do not belong to the body," it would not for that reason stop being part of the body. If the whole body were an eye, where would the sense of hearing be? If the whole body were an ear, where would the sense of smell be? But in fact God has placed the parts in the body, every one of them, just as he wanted them to be. If they were all one part, where would the body be? As it is, there are many parts, but one body.

The eye cannot say to the hand, "I don't need you!" And the head cannot say to the feet, "I don't need you!" On the contrary, those parts of the body that seem to be weaker are indispensable, and the parts that we think are less honorable we treat with special honor. And the parts that are unpresentable are treated with special modesty, while our presentable parts need no special treatment. But God has put the body together, giving greater honor to the parts that lacked it, so that there should be no division in the body, but that its parts should have equal concern for each other. If one part suffers, every part suffers with it; if one part is honored, every part rejoices with it.

Now you are the body of Christ, and each one of you is a part of it. And God has placed in the church first of all apostles, second prophets, third teachers, then miracles, then gifts of healing, of helping, of guidance, and of different kinds of tongues. Are all apostles? Are all prophets? Are all teachers? Do all work miracles? Do all have gifts of healing? Do all speak in tongues? Do all interpret? Now eagerly desire the greater gifts. (1 Cor 12:4-31)

A first-century reader or listener hearing an analogy to the "body" might immediately think of it in reference to the "body politic" in Rome.[5] As Julia Mebane describes in *The Body Politic in Roman Political Thought*, "By the end of the Julio-Claudian era, the *res publica* had been radically reimagined as a collection of limbs and organs unable to survive without a head to command it." The Roman Empire occupied diverse cultures that were immediately assimilated into Roman culture, and assimilation equaled allegiance. The head (Rome) determined which limbs and organs were vital to survival and which were dispensable in the collective. In contrast to the Roman approach, Paul taught the Corinthian churches what it means to have allegiance to Christ as the head of the body. As part of the body of Christ, they were called to treat each member as important and indispensable; in addition, they were to have equal concern for each other, participating in one another's suffering and rejoicing (1 Cor 12:26). Paul paints the unity of the church, amid an occupying empire, as pivotal in proclaiming Christ as the head who includes and respects all people in God's kingdom. The body of Christ was to directly contend against the body of empire.

The temple imagery from Romans 12 and the body imagery from 1 Corinthians 12 provide a model for the unity of Jesus followers. Paul was certain that unity would be experienced (1) as God's indwelling presence with us if we lived as though we belong to one another (Rom 12:5). In 1 Corinthians 12:26 Paul envisions unity (2) as a countercultural resistance to empire achieved by leading lives of concern for one another.

UNITY IN EPHESIANS 4

In the epistle to the Jesus communities in Ephesus, the apostle Paul wrote to one of the largest cultural epicenters of polytheism where, surprisingly, one of the strongest and fastest-growing church communities in the first century resided. And he wrote while imprisoned for the gospel (for which he eventually was executed). What kind of letter would be written by a leader near the end of his ministry to one of the most mature faith communities of that time? Paul writes to them about unity. In the first half of his letter, he reminds them that the gospel story is about how God has established a multicultural and unified new humanity through the life, death, and resurrection of Christ. The second half of Ephesians, where our passage begins, focuses on how we as the church ought to respond to God's story. Paul begins by emphasizing unity through the word *one*: "one body," "one Spirit," "one hope," "one Lord," "one faith," "one baptism," and "one God." Paul writes,

> As a prisoner for the Lord, then, I urge you to live a life worthy of the calling you have received. Be completely humble and gentle; be patient, bearing with one another in love. Make every effort to keep the unity of the Spirit through the bond of peace. There is one body and one Spirit, just as you were called to one hope when you were called; one Lord, one faith, one baptism; one God and Father of all, who is over all and through all and in all.
>
> But to each one of us grace has been given as Christ apportioned it. This is why it says:
>
> "When he ascended on high,
>   he took many captives
>   and gave gifts to his people."
>
> (What does "he ascended" mean except that he also descended to the lower, earthly regions? He who descended is the very one who ascended higher than all the heavens, in order to fill the whole universe.) So Christ himself gave the apostles, the prophets, the

evangelists, the [shepherds][6] and teachers, to equip his people for works of service, so that the body of Christ may be built up until we all reach unity in the faith and in the knowledge of the Son of God and become mature, attaining to the whole measure of the fullness of Christ.

Then we will no longer be infants, tossed back and forth by the waves, and blown here and there by every wind of teaching and by the cunning and craftiness of people in their deceitful scheming. Instead, speaking the truth in love, we will grow to become in every respect the mature body of him who is the head, that is, Christ. From him the whole body, joined and held together by every supporting ligament, grows and builds itself up in love, as each part does its work. (Eph 4:1-16)

In this late letter to a mature Jesus community, Paul uses two metaphors almost like shorthand for the themes of temple and body. When Paul uses the phrase "built up" or "builds itself up" (Eph 4:12, 16), the reader is reminded of earlier in Ephesians where he describes the unity of a diverse community as a temple or dwelling place for God's presence.

Consequently, you are no longer foreigners and strangers, but fellow citizens with God's people and also members of his household, *built* on the foundation of the apostles and prophets, with Christ Jesus himself as the chief cornerstone. In him the whole *building* is joined together and rises to become a *holy temple* in the Lord. And in him you too are being *built* together to become a *dwelling* in which God lives by his Spirit. (Eph 2:19-22, italics mine)

When Paul uses phrases like "one body" or "body of Christ" or "whole body" (Eph 4:4, 12, 16), he is again describing the unity of a diverse community as a body, with Christ as the head instead of Rome as the head. In addition, Ephesians 4 highlights the telos of unity, or the result of unity. The maturity process of the church is to reach unity through Jesus and become "the whole measure of the fullness of Christ" (Eph 4:13):

communally, to be completely like Christ. In Ephesians 4:14-16, Paul seems to emphasize the main point again, that "we will no longer be infants" (Eph 4:14) but mature "in love" (Eph 4:16). The church reaches maturity by achieving unity through Jesus, which is defined by working together within our diversity, with love for one another.

UNITY IN JOHN 17

Why does Paul repeatedly emphasize the importance of unity to a diverse set of Christians? When we read Paul's underscoring of unity, we can't help but see how much this leader was influenced by Jesus' own attention to the unity of all believers. Jesus prays in John 17:20-23,

> My prayer is not for them [the disciples] alone. I pray also for those who will believe in me through their message, that all of them may be one, Father, just as you are in me and I am in you. May they also be in us so that the world may believe that you have sent me. I have given them the glory that you gave me, that they may be one as we are one—I in them and you in me—so that they may be brought to complete unity. Then the world will know that you sent me and have loved them even as you have loved me.

Christine Pohl says of this prayer, "The best testimony to the truth of the gospel is the quality of our life together. Jesus risked his reputation and the credibility of his story by tying them to how his followers live and care for one another in community."[7]

Unity displays to the larger community the full reflection of Christ. The unity of a diverse new humanity who love and are committed to one another in the beautiful work of self-giving love to our city, community, and neighborhood is how we communally imitate Jesus. This answers how the community of Jesus will fulfill Christ's call—"Love each other" (Jn 15:17). This shows the world who he is by the ways we engage with one another, how we work together, in love, through our many differences. This takes a special kind of leadership, a leadership that comes with the promise that we will one day work ourselves out of a job. It contrasts with contemporary culture surrounding the church throughout time, modeling a better kind of leadership.

UNITY AND APEST

In Acts 15, we see the unity of the church threatened in a way that most of us in the current American polarized society can resonate with. But the outcome of the council at Jerusalem is far from what we would expect based on our post-pandemic divisions. There was unity in the church, led by a collaborative work of different APEST leaders. This biblical text shows us that there were teachers, evangelists, apostles, shepherds, and prophets who were all included in this lengthy and thoughtful process to discern and lead the church together (Acts 15:1, 3, 4, 6, 32, respectively). If not for this kind of collaborative shared leadership, the first-century church might have prevented Jews and Gentiles from following Jesus. The apostle Paul worked collaboratively with other leaders to share with the Jesus communities in Galatia, "So in Christ Jesus you are all children of God through faith, for all of you who were baptized into Christ have clothed yourselves with Christ. There is neither Jew nor Gentile, neither slave nor free, nor is there male and female, for you are all one in Christ Jesus" (Gal 3:26-28).

Neil Cole writes of APEST,

Individually, these gifts reflect parts of a whole that, when seen together, manifests the full image of God and the full measure of Jesus Christ. It is only when *all* these gifts are released to function naturally in the body and they mature to the point of *equipping others* that the church will fully reflect Jesus—in all His beauty—to the world. In order for this to happen, we must first discern what these gifts are, understand that they are still active today, and rediscover how they are intended to work together to accomplish God's purpose here on earth. In isolation from one another, the embers will remain dormant; but drawn together in unity of purpose, they await only the wind of the Holy Spirit to fan them into full flame.[8]

In order to reframe APEST with a lens toward sharing leadership, we need to keep in mind that these gifts are embedded within the fuller picture of a mature people of God. The purpose of the gifts enumerated in APEST is to represent God's presence with us and Jesus' kingdom (his rule and reign) as flourishing for our cities, communities, and neighborhoods. This goal will only be realized with sharing leadership.

REFRAMING APOSTLE, PROPHET, EVANGELIST, SHEPHERD, AND TEACHER LEADERS

*I can do things you cannot, you can do things
I cannot; together we can do great things.*

MOTHER TERESA

*Very truly I tell you, unless a kernel of wheat falls to the ground and dies,
it remains only a single seed. But if it dies, it produces many seeds.*

JOHN 12:24

THE SETTING WAS FALL OF 2020. Restaurants were shifting to sidewalk cafés with newly purchased heating lamps or clear-plastic tents. Offices had shifted to working from home, severely testing the viability of remote work. Schools and school board discussions were heated regarding whether to host in-person, virtual, or hybrid classrooms. ICU beds in hospitals were still taxed from the Covid-19 pandemic. In addition, the pandemic was exacerbated by a drastic increase in both mental health and domestic violence crises.[1] It took a monumental toll on the female workforce.[2] The world witnessed Black Lives Matter protests in the wake of George Floyd's death, neo-Nazism efforts, and anti-Asian hate crimes.[3] In the United States, the November 2020 presidential election was looming. It's stated that the country had never been more divided than at that time.[4]

In the church world, while pastors and leaders were scrambling to shift from in-person worship services to streaming services, we were also bracing ourselves for the political angst that occurs every four years in the United States. "In 1963, the Rev. Dr. Martin Luther King Jr. said, 'It is appalling that the most segregated hour of Christian America is 11 o'clock on Sunday morning' and, according to experts, that assertion remains true today."[5] While he was referring to racial segregation between Black and White Americans, the sentiment seemed to apply in 2020 (and some would argue continues to today) to a political-party divide that existed in the pews that fall.

I remember speaking to one Asian American leader from Chicago who served a predominantly White church that he and his mixed-race family loved and had served in for decades. Over dinner, he shared with me how political turmoil throttled the life of his church. After what seemed like unending meetings and conversations to reconcile the divide, he and his family ultimately left the church. This is just one of hundreds of stories I've heard of church leaders experiencing such disunity during that time. Barna reported in October 2020, a month prior to the election, that most leaders felt the pressures of navigating the political divide along with all its associated moral and social issues from "people *inside* their church— not outside."[6]

It is a miraculous statement, but in our local church that fall we did not experience one political schism. It wasn't because we didn't have disagreements around politics and social policy; we had our fair share. Neither was it because we live in Hawaii, the Aloha State; we also had our fair share of masking/nonmasking, vaccine or no vaccine protests, Black Lives Matter and White Lives Matter protests, and Biden versus Trump rallies. Our church avoided division because of two mature leaders.

Hanzo, who is a mature Teacher in the APEST gifting, named the concerns during this heated season openly, peacefully, and neutrally. He began equipping our main leaders to have conversations instead of debates, remembering that the kingdom of God runs primarily through unity not uniformity.[7] Because every disciple in our congregation was already well

versed in our discipleship essential of thick community, committed to relation building, truth telling, and peacemaking, we could have these conversations. As a Teacher, Hanzo asked the community to revisit our
commitments to one another, to choose to trust one another instead of
being suspicious of one another, to speak honestly with grace and love
instead of withholding information or feelings from others, and to help
create safe environments for dialogue instead of breeding divisive and resentful thoughts. Hanzo equipped the church to commit to unity through
thick community.

Meli, who is a mature Prophet in the APEST gifting, equipped our local
community to respond to what was happening in our world, locally, na-
tionally, and globally, with lament. In preparation for our public gathering
that fall, she equipped our leaders to lead the community through liturgy,
prayers of lament, song, and hope. With this approach they could draw our
community's attention to both the suffering they experienced and to the
God who can hear and act upon our suffering. She equipped our church
to remember that lamenting is a "stark reminder that suffering is not a
passing condition that provides a mere bump in the road toward celebration, . . . suffering has a direction and purpose, [and] . . . suffering is
not glossed over but embraces as a necessary part of worship."[8] The whole
community, both Christians and non-Christians, was invited to grieve
together, with and for one another. They grieved through reflection and
contemplation; listening to words spoken in native Hawaiian, the language
of a people group who understand deeply suffering and loss; and praying
together words of lamentation that named suffering and loss locally and
globally. Meli equipped the church to commit to unity through lament.

Both a mature Teacher and a mature Prophet leader helped to equip the
church to be more Christlike through their commitment to unity.

EPHESIANS 4 AND APEST

In Ephesians 4, Paul addresses the maturity of the people of God through
unity not uniformity. Keeping that in mind, we will now look at the portion
that introduces APEST, namely Ephesians 4:11-13,

So Christ himself gave the apostles, the prophets, the evangelists, the [shepherds] and teachers, to equip his people for works of service, so that the body of Christ may be built up until we all reach unity in the faith and in the knowledge of the Son of God and become mature, attaining to the whole measure of the fullness of Christ.

While there has been much written on the topic of APEST, I want to provide some guideposts for how I will use APEST as a framework to consider sharing leadership over hierarchical or flat leadership.

1. Equipping. One of the unresolved debates about APEST gifting is whether it is just for leaders or for everyone. I will keep us in the lane of APEST as leadership gifting, mainly because it has to do with equipping the people of God for works of service in order for the whole church to become more like Christ together. The emphasis that delineates leadership will be that of equipping the church.

To equip is defined as to "supply with the necessary items for a particular purpose" or "prepare someone for a particular task."[9] The Greek word used in Ephesians 4:12, *katartismos,* is often translated "perfecting" or "complete furnishing."[10] This is the only time the word is used in the Bible, so when we look at its verbal counterpart, *katartizō,* we find that a more robust definition is "render" ("cause to become"[11]), "fit out, equip, put in order, arrange or adjust," "strengthen or make one what they ought to be." Hebrews 13:21, in fact, also uses *katartizō:*

Make you perfect [*katartizō*] in every good work to do his will, working in you that which is well pleasing in his sight, through Jesus Christ; to whom be glory for ever and ever. Amen. (KJV)

NIV translates the same words as "equip you with everything good for doing his will, and may he work in us what is pleasing to him, through Jesus Christ, to whom be glory for ever and ever. Amen."

We can clearly see that the equipping work of leaders is not isolated to instructing or completing tasks for others; it's heavily involved in preparing and supplying what the people of God need. The job of the leader is to equip (prepare, supply, strengthen, help them become) the people of God for works of service that contribute to unity and congregational maturity.

2. Maturity over rank. While it's also debatable whether there is a certain "ranking" or "prioritization" of the Apostles, Prophets, Evangelists, Shepherds, and Teachers, I will have us focus on Paul's emphasis in Ephesians 4:1-10, which is not on rank but on mature people who are:

- Disciples, living a life worthy of imitating Jesus (Eph 4:1)
- Marked by humility, gentleness, patience, forbearance, and love (Eph 4:2)
- Committed to unity (Eph 4:3-6)
- Following Christ into self-emptying/*kenōsis* (Eph 4:9-10)

The first ten verses of Ephesians 4 are reminiscent of the first element of mature leadership, which I discussed in chapter four: Christlike humility. Once again, the kenotic journey of the leader imitating the kenotic journey of Christ, highlighted in Philippians 2:5-11, is brought to the forefront as we examine how Christ descended before ascending. If unity and maturity of the church are attained through the life and love of Christ, then it serves us well to consider how Christ lived and loved. Without a full understanding of the marks of mature leadership (Christlike humility that leads to hospitality then to honor and finally to hope), we could easily perceive APEST as a prescription for dominance.

I wonder often about the last conversation Jesus had with his disciples, the people he knew would be the leaders to help launch a new humanity. What would be the final instructions I would want to give as I pass off the role and responsibilities of leadership to the next crew of people. I would imagine spending the most time on the priorities of leadership, maintaining the organizational structure, and clarifying the vision toward a sustainable future: Boss Work 101. Instead, Jesus says,

> My command is this: Love each other as I have loved you. Greater love has no one than this: to lay down one's life for one's friends. You are my friends if you do what I command. I no longer call you

servants, because a servant does not know his master's business. Instead, I have called you friends, for everything that I learned from my Father I have made known to you. You did not choose me, but I chose you and appointed you so that you might go and bear fruit— fruit that will last—and so that whatever you ask in my name the Father will give you. This is my command: Love each other. (Jn 15:12-17)

In preparing his disciples, Jesus emphasizes their identity—defined by their intimacy with, proximity to, and reliance on Jesus—and their purpose—to love one another in a way that imitates the way Jesus loves, bears lasting fruit, and is self-giving.

It's important to keep in mind that APEST is a framework for understanding how sharing leadership operates outside of rank but inside of gifting.

3. Gifting over role. It's also debated whether the last two giftings, Shepherd and Teacher, are one gifting or separate giftings. There is reason to believe that the Shepherd-Teacher, or more popularly pastor-teacher, can be one gifting, but here I will separate the two so that there's clarity about how each contributes to unity and communal maturity differently. It also helps us to distance ourselves from cultural connotations of pastor-teacher as an elevated job description in the church (as evidenced by the power pressures discussed in chaps. 2 and 3). I believe the more familiar grouping is the role of pastor-preacher and not the leadership gifts of Shepherd and Teacher.

The pastor-preacher is a job description most churches use in calling a new senior pastor. It's an expectation that the role and responsibility will meet two needs: establish their ideal community through social availability (without the ability to challenge the congregants) and increase numerical church attendance through sermons (without the ability to change systems). The two leadership giftings of Shepherd and Teacher exist to equip the people of God for works of service and contribute to unity and Christlikeness in the church (see fig. 6.1).

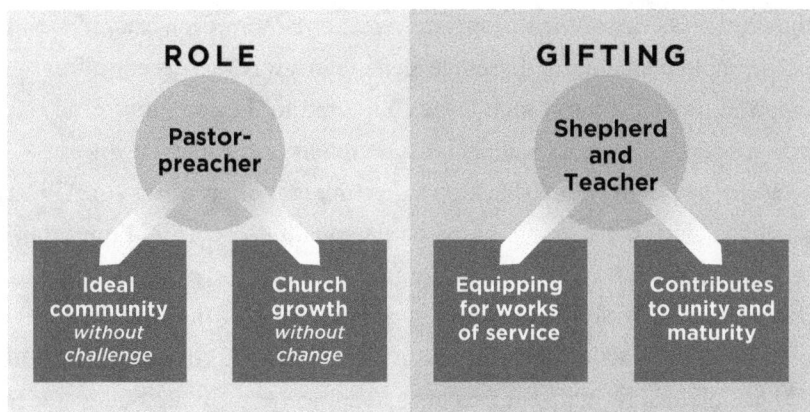

ROLE		GIFTING	
Pastor-preacher		**Shepherd and Teacher**	
Ideal community *without challenge*	Church growth *without change*	Equipping for works of service	Contributes to unity and maturity

Figure 6.1. Difference between pastor-preacher role and Shepherd and Teacher gifting

4. Real people. I capitalize the leadership giftings (Apostle, Prophet, Evangelist, Shepherd, Teacher), not because these hold any more prominence over other roles or work in the church but to remind us that each leadership gifting stands for the name of a person, each one full of unique complexities, journeys, glory, and brokenness. While we will be discussing these as leadership gifting in the church, without naming real people in actual roles, I can at best make generic observations and recommendations around each gifting. I cannot include all the characteristics each leader brings to the table with his or her individual personality, history, values, beliefs, joys, trauma, and layers of culture. That being said, I will address APEST in the context of gender, race, and culture in chapter eight in order to expand an existing APEST conversation that has often left out marginalized or disempowered people.

5. Tool not test. Finally, while we live in a world where personality and temperaments are highly consumed, we are not treating APEST as another personality test for personal consumption. We are simply using it as a tool to understand sharing leadership in the church. With the continual headlines describing domineering leadership and failure of leadership in the church, most work offering an antidote to this culture has focused solely on the health, soul care, or personality type of the main leader. There is an acute need to furnish an approach to leadership apart from hierarchical or flat leadership.

There have been many attempts at describing shared leadership and how sharing leadership can operate in the church, the strongest being APEST in the church-planting and missional movements. However, few examples exist of the implementation of sharing leadership in a way that decentralizes the pulpit in order for the church to be connected to the community, depicts how it operates in praxis, and includes an intentional variety of voices.

Many books examine sharing leadership, including works on APEST and even church leadership based on personality types (e.g., Enneagram, StrengthsFinder, etc.). But there is a need for a real-life model depicting distributed leadership embedded in the structure of the church and explaining its impact on the community it serves. APEST is most helpful when explained through the lens of gender, race, and culture that includes women and men, BIPOC leaders, and the local community.

THE PURPOSE OF APEST

As we can clearly see from Ephesians 4, the purpose of APEST leadership is to equip. What does it equip the church to do? Works of service (Eph 4:12). And how do we know that the people of God are being equipped? They experience unity, not uniformity, and communal maturity or Christlikeness (Eph 4:13). We can also see clearly that APEST leadership does not perform the works of service alone; this requires "the whole body" (Eph 4: 16). In addition, growth is not judged by numerical growth but by how well the people of God, as they serve and work together, experience unity and maturity—how well the church reflects the fullness of Christ. Who is it reflected to? Or in other words, who benefits from their unity and maturity? It's the community the church resides in (see fig. 6.2).

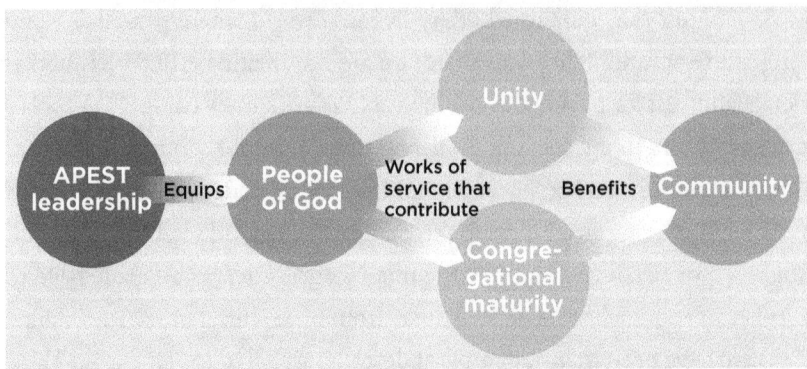

Figure 6.2. Purpose of APEST leadership

In contrast, most churches consider a different set of responsibilities and metrics for leadership. The purpose of the pastor-preacher is to instruct. What do they instruct the church to do? Have an individualistic, consumeristic, homogeneous faith. What's the metric used to see that this is happening? Church numerical growth and an ideal community. Who does it benefit? It benefits the church itself (see fig. 6.3).

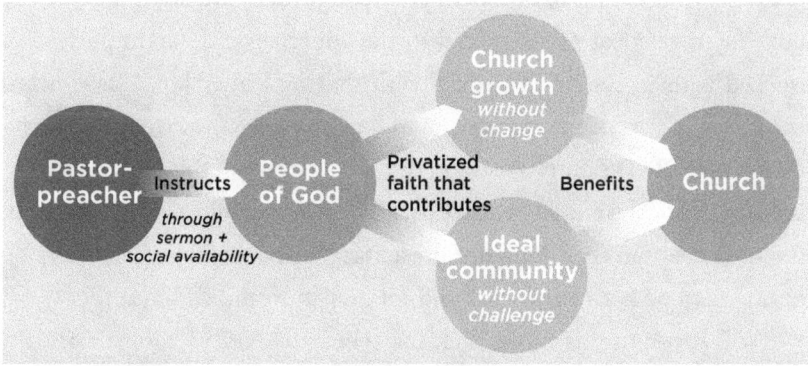

Figure 6.3. Purpose of pastor-preacher leadership

The reflective work to do now in connecting APEST to sharing leadership is to see just how each of the leadership giftings operates. How does each gifting, Apostle, Prophet, Evangelist, Shepherd, and Teacher, equip the people of God for works of service that contribute to unity and congregational maturity that benefits the community?

A different way to answer these questions is to think about establishing a specific environment that equips the people of God. The mature Apostle values a sending environment and equips the people of God to live out their calling for the sake of the community. The mature Prophet values a liberating environment and equips the people of God to pursue God's shalom within the congregation and community. The mature Evangelist values a welcoming environment and equips the people of God to live out the gospel with and for the community. The mature Shepherd values a healing environment and equips the people of God to seek wholeness and holiness together and be reconciled to the community. The mature Teacher values a learning environment and equips the people of God to learn from one another and invite the community into God's story.

THE LIMITS OF APEST

While we are highlighting APEST as a tool for sharing leadership to establish an environment of flourishing in our churches and communities, this in no way claims to be a perfect or complete model for leadership. In both my own local ministry and in the churches and communities I've worked with to clarify and equip with sharing leadership, I have heard countless stories of harm, hurts, and hardships encountered when navigating APEST. The emphasis should not be placed on this tool; instead, it is best to concentrate on the maturity of the leadership. As we will see in the next chapter, the immature presentation of each of these leadership giftings can be harmful to both the congregation and community.

I will speak to this more later, but when the APEST tool is not used wisely, it can thrust a congregation into experiences of offense, envy, resentment, competition, and shame. I've seen, including within my own congregation, Apostles and Prophets lording it over others because of their sense of urgency and perfectionism that excludes the congregation. Shepherds and Teachers can become suspicious of others and any resistance to movement. Evangelists can become chained to the crowd.

I believe that using APEST as a tool can help us develop better and clearer ways to be committed to unity and maturity. In my own local church, even before we launched our first public gathering, we used APEST to clearly commit ourselves to one another—so that we could face the inevitable challenges of diversity and differing preferences. I led our initial team through a simple exercise to help them preemptively name some challenges and linked those challenges to some inescapable feelings.

Our launch ministry was planned as a basic weekly potluck community dinner. Easy. Set up some tables and chairs in a nearby community room, minimal decor needed, a rotation of people signing up to provide a main dish for the week, and invite friends, family, neighbors, and coworkers to share what it means to be present with one another and present in the community around us. Simple. The simplicity was on purpose because it allowed space for my leadership team to be able to reflect from the beginning on our differences in preferences based on our APEST.

The Teachers could point out something wrong with the community dinner because it didn't have a visible spot for Scripture to be taught. We worked on the Teachers connecting to Jesus during this experimental launch season, knowing that he is the incarnate Word that never returns empty. The Shepherds noticed that the community dinners could be threatened by growing too quickly and people being left behind. We navigated with the Shepherds on connecting with Jesus, knowing that he knows every person's name and needs and is providing care for each of them already. The Evangelists felt anxious that if the community dinners didn't work or if the team didn't put in the work to invite guests, then new people wouldn't come. We encouraged the Evangelists to connect with Jesus, knowing that he values not just those who are new or far from him but also those who are close to him. The Prophets knew that they would feel grumpy because community dinners just didn't cut it in terms of addressing real community justice needs. We prayed with the Prophets that connecting to Jesus meant knowing that his kingdom is always pursuing righteousness through his people experiencing communal life together. And I, as the lone Apostle (at the beginning), shared with the team that I may feel antsy at times because just hosting weekly community dinners week in and week out would feel so plodding, offering no movement forward. But my commitment to them was that I would connect to Jesus knowing that his kingdom is on the move and that it often starts small and slowly before expanding exponentially.

We left that final prep time as a team of people, different in so many ways, excited for the work of service at hand, and feeling more clearly how we were committing ourselves to Jesus and to one another. From that first year of simple weekly community dinners, we have multiplied seven years later into twelve different missional communities. Our diverse leadership has established environments of sending, liberating, welcoming, healing, and learning to equip the people of God in the works of service for the benefit of the community around us, ministering to the needs of over 650 persons.

7

RELYING ON APEST FOR SHARING LEADERSHIP

Great leaders do not create followers, they create more leaders.

TOM PETERS

Walking along the beach of Lake Galilee, Jesus saw two brothers: Simon (later called Peter) and Andrew. They were fishing, throwing their nets into the lake. It was their regular work. Jesus said to them, "Come with me. I'll make a new kind of fisherman out of you. I'll show you how to catch men and women instead of perch and bass." They didn't ask questions, but simply dropped their nets and followed.

MATTHEW 4:18-20 THE MESSAGE

I REMEMBER WHEN APEST was first introduced to me. My three-person pastoral team for our local church plant at that time was taking a seminar on polycentric leadership run by Alan Hirsch's team in the first decade of the twenty-first century. His book *The Forgotten Ways: Reactivating the Missional Church* had recently come out, so we had wanted to learn about best practices for sharing leadership.[1] Despite the goal of wanting to share church leadership together, the whole conversation felt uncomfortable, as though it was elevating the Apostle gifting over the others, mainly over the Shepherd and Teacher leadership gifting. It left one of our leaders, who is a Shepherd leader, to feel undermined and undervalued. It also misled the two Apostle leaders, including myself, to believe that we were better leaders simply because we were Apostle leaders.

Fast forward to my tenure in a three-person executive team for an international church-planting organization, where we spoke often of our emphasis on promoting polycentric leadership. We again participated in training on APEST and sharing leadership, but we couldn't ever be quite sure how it actually works in the church. In any event, the organization's culture clearly prized the Apostle leadership gifting, and even made certain Apostle leaders exempt from some responsibilities because they didn't "fit."

That local church plant no longer exists after its leadership cultivated an environment in which Shepherd leaders continued to view Apostle leaders as threats. That international church-planting organization is on the decline with the original leadership still in place, claiming that they have not expanded because other leaders lack "unconscious competence." Without putting in the work to utilize APEST as a meaningful and sustainable tool, most churches and organizations don't share leadership. Instead, they can easily misuse APEST as a tool to perpetuate hierarchical leadership.

While there are quite a few writings on APEST, they have been limited in illustrating how to actually draw on the gifts of APEST to sustainably lead a church or community. How does APEST work effectively (and in real life) in sharing leadership? While in the next chapter, we will look at reframing APEST to include all types of leaders (gender, race, and culture), in this chapter, we'll first look at what each APEST gifting values and how APEST is used as a tool for sharing leadership.

APEST AND VALUES

What the leader values shapes how and why they lead. Each APEST leader prizes something as more valuable. For a community of Jesus followers to mature, (1) each APEST leader must nurture a particular kind of environment in order to equip the people of God to contribute to communal unity and maturity, and (2) each must be given latitude to apply their individual giftings to benefit both the congregation and the community it serves.

- The Teacher values learning and the people of God inhabiting the incarnational Word of God.

- The Shepherd values healing and the people of God seeking the wholeness and holiness of a God community.

- The Evangelist values welcoming and the people of God living as the incarnation of the good news of the kingdom of God.

- The Prophet values liberating and the people of God pursuing God's shalom within the congregation and with the community it resides in.

- The Apostle values sending and the people of God living out their calling for the sake of their community, city, and neighborhood—the *imago Dei* (bearers of God's image) being sent by the *missio Dei* (the missional, sending God).

A different way to think of what each APEST values is to recognize the kind of communal environment each leader desires to establish. The Teacher establishes a learning environment, the Shepherd a healing environment, the Evangelist a welcoming environment, the Prophet a liberating environment, and the Apostle a sending environment. A community that exists within the loving leadership that establishes all these environments will mature together to be Christlike for the sake of the world around them (see table 7.1).

Table 7.1. The APEST leader's value and communal environment

APEST	Value	Communal environment
Apostle	The people of God living out their calling of being sent	Sending
Prophet	The people of God pursuing God's shalom within the congregation and with the community in which it resides	Liberating
Evangelist	The people of God living as the incarnation of the good news of the kingdom of God	Welcoming
Shepherd	The people of God seeking the wholeness and holiness of a God community	Healing
Teacher	The people of God inhabiting the Word of God and God's story	Learning

Having acknowledged what each APEST values, it is helpful also to identify the maturity level of the leader. In part one, we looked at how the procession from humility to honor to hospitality to hope marks the maturity level of a leader. Each leader's environment can be established well—compassionately, thoughtfully, intentionally, and sustainably—according to each APEST leader's maturity. Having attained humility, a leader will honor the community being led and the leadership team, offer hospitality to both the congregation and the larger community, and be hopeful of the community flourishing. Along the way, each APEST leader's value will look different according to the leader's level of maturity.

APEST AND MATURITY

Missiologist Lesslie Newbigin writes,

> The task of ministry is to lead the congregation as a whole in a mission to the community as a whole, to claim its whole public life, as well as the personal lives of all its people, for God's rule. It means equipping all the members of the congregation to understand and fulfill their several roles in this mission through their faithfulness in their daily work. It means training and equipping them to be active followers of Jesus in his assault on the principalities and powers which he has disarmed on his cross. And it means sustaining them in bearing the cost of that warfare.[2]

For clarity, we will use Newbigin's terms to delineate which people we are referring to: *congregation* to refer to a group of Christ followers (the church) and *community* to refer to the neighborhood, city, or community in which the church resides. Note that maturity always moves the congregation to the community. Mature APEST leadership never exists just for the sake of an isolated congregation. APEST leaders together shape and equip the ecclesia to participate with God in the renewal of all things.

The task of ministry through APEST is "to equip his people for works of service, so that the body of Christ may be built up until we all reach unity in the faith and in the knowledge of the Son of God and become mature, attaining to the whole measure of the fullness of Christ" (Eph 4:12-13). The APEST approach equips the congregation as a whole for "works of service" to the community as a whole. This work of connecting formation to mission, the congregation's identity to its purpose, is what brings about both unity and maturity, enabling the community around it to flourish.

The mature Teacher equips the congregation to inhabit the incarnate Word of God so that the congregation not only teaches one another what it means to live into God's future in an everyday way but also invites the community to join in God's story. The mature Shepherd equips the congregation to seek wholeness and holiness together, with and for one another, in order to embody reconciliation between the congregation and the community. The mature Evangelist equips the congregation to live incarnationally with and for the community to extend the table of fellowship to all, particularly those who are far from the rest of society. The mature Prophet equips the congregation to pursue God's shalom (renewal, liberation, right relationship with others and with God) personally, within the congregation and with the community. The mature Apostle equips the congregation to live out its calling, which means being sent out together for the flourishing of the community (see table 7.2).

Table 7.2. APEST immaturity and maturity

APEST	Value	Immaturity	Maturity
Apostle	Sending	Competitive environment	Equips the congregation to live out its calling for the sake of the community
Prophet	Liberating	Perfect environment	Equips the congregation to pursue God's shalom within the congregation and with the community
Evangelist	Welcoming	Entertaining environment	Equips the congregation to live out the gospel with and for the community
Shepherd	Healing	Comfortable environment	Equips the congregation to seek wholeness and holiness together and be reconciled to the community
Teacher	Learning	Teaching environment	Equips the congregation to teach and learn from one another and invite the community into God's story

Immaturity often means that the individual leader, or just the congregation, is disconnected from the community. Or, if the community is involved, it may be exploited and ministry done *to* it instead of for and with it. The APEST leader grows and matures through the four Hs—humility, honor, hospitality, and hope—by connecting to Jesus.

How then does this movement from immaturity to maturity occur? While immaturity is often treated as a lack of knowledge or skill, I think that in leadership it results from a failure to name the motivating factor: What's really in the heart behind the immaturity? If maturity is a natural and grace-filled process of growth, then we need to recognize natural points that move us from immaturity to maturity. Natural progress often results in the midst of fear and loss.

Immature Teachers fear being incorrect in handling God's word, so they overcorrect the congregation. Immature Shepherds feel threatened by change and the possible loss of belonging, so they overprotect the congregation. Immature Evangelists fear criticism and rejection, so they overplease the congregation. Immature Prophets fear sinfulness, so they may react with anger toward the congregation. Immature Apostles fear stagnation, so they become bored and resentful of the congregation.

The immature Teacher is often thinking about creating a teaching environment instead of a learning environment—focusing on the Bible being taught correctly and publicly in the congregation and limiting the number of people who are considered qualified to teach. The mature Teacher moves from being an Expert to being a Facilitator. Facilitators follow Jesus, our Great Teacher. This kind of mature Teacher is filled with compassion for the people and is able to gauge the learning pace, capacity, and capability of the people. A mature Teacher avoids overcorrection and encourages communal learning, which leads to reflection, practice, and transformation. The mature Teacher wants people to experience the mercy of Christ in the incarnate Word and not just the words of the Bible.

The immature Shepherd is often thinking about creating a comfortable environment instead of a healing environment—focusing on making sure that nothing, including challenge, conflict, new people, or disruptive personalities, can threaten the current group's comfortability. An immature Shepherd may expect to be the congregation's "first call" and tends toward overprotection. Maturity occurs when the Shepherd moves from being a Best Friend to being a Nurse. Nurses understand Jesus, our Great Physician, and his diagnosis and healing power. This kind of mature Shepherd tends to people's needs with a focus toward communal health and interdependence and an expectation that the road to healing comes with bumps and dis-ease. The mature Shepherd wants people to experience Love-become-flesh.

The immature Evangelist is often thinking about creating an entertaining environment instead of a welcoming environment—focusing on making sure that the event is attractive enough to capture the community's attention and draw a crowd. The immature Evangelist is hopeful that the event will grow, consequently avoiding rejection by overappeasing. Maturity occurs when the Evangelist moves from being an Entertainer/Event Planner to a Connector/Bridge Builder, providing a welcoming environment to connect the community to Jesus our Great Host. This mature Evangelist offers a bridge from the community to Jesus' family and from the congregation to the ones Jesus seeks.

The immature Prophet is often thinking about creating a perfect environment instead of a liberating environment—focusing on doing things according to rules instead of relationships. An immature Prophet often expects perfect behavior and response, leading to anger when disappointed. Maturity occurs when the Prophet moves from being a Critic to being an Optometrist/Eye Doctor. Optometrists know that fixing our eyes on Jesus, the author and perfecter of our faith, is the only way that people will recognize and be transformed to right living and seek justice with mercy. The mature Prophet will correct our vision so we experience Jesus' beauty, truth, justice, peace, righteousness, wholeness, faithfulness, and sincere love, moving a congregation toward God and community.

The immature Apostle is often thinking about creating a competitive environment instead of a sending environment—focusing on winning, even seeking to secure the end by any means. An immature Apostle assumes that bearing fruit is the most important goal and strongly resists "stagnation." Maturity occurs when the Apostle moves from being a Winner to being a Pacer. A Pacer knows to run just a little farther ahead so the following runners can see how fast they should run and how much farther there is to go. A mature Apostle experiences the deep patience and long-suffering of Christ. The mature Apostle wants people to experience Jesus, who emptied himself, offering the prize Paul promises for all of us: "I press on toward the goal to win the prize for which God has called me heavenward in Christ Jesus" (Phil 3:14).

See table 7.3 for a comparison of mature and immature APEST leaders.

Table 7.3. Heart behind the immature APEST and connection to Jesus

APEST	Value	Immaturity	Feeling to avoid	Reaction to congregation	Connection to Jesus	Maturity
Apostle	Sending	Winner	Stagnant	Resentful of	Patience > impatience	Pacer
Prophet	Liberating	Critic	Unholy	Angry with	Gentleness > disappointment	Optometrist/ eye doctor
Evangelist	Welcoming	Entertainer/ event planner	Rejected	Overappease	Faithfulness > anxiousness	Connector/ bridge builder
Shepherd	Healing	Best friend	Threatened	Overprotect	Love > loneliness	Nurse
Teacher	Learning	Expert	Wrong	Overcorrect	Mercy > judgment	Facilitator

APEST AND SHARING LEADERSHIP: STRUCTURE

The intricacies of APEST can be a powerful tool in developing shared leadership. Sharing leadership and drawing on the gifts of each APEST leader helps the congregation to be fully equipped into the mission and likeness of Christ, and ultimately to be connected to the community. Mature APEST leaders realize that they can only lead through sharing leadership.

Continuing in Newbigin's vision for the church, that the whole of the congregation be equipped to live for the flourishing of the whole of the community, we can examine (1) where APEST sits in the structure of the church and the community and (2) how each gift's engagement with time (rhythm) is incorporated into the work of leadership. While the Teacher and Shepherd leaders sit in the depth of the congregation, the Evangelist leader sits at the border of the congregation and community, and both the Prophet and Apostle leaders sit outside the border into the community (see fig. 7.1). Why?

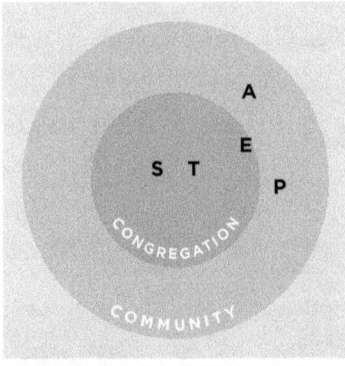

Figure 7.1. Structure of APEST

Since the gifts of the Teacher and Shepherd leaders can equip the congregation to dig deeply into their faith, both the learning and healing environments are hosted by these two types of Christ followers. The community requires digging and excavating to become a family that practices mutual learning and growth. And this must take place in a safe and sacred space that allows for healing and belonging. Otherwise, the work is shallow. The Teacher's and Shepherd's eyes are on the congregation.

The gift of the Evangelist leader is to equip the congregation for connection to the community, where it's a two-way street, moving foot traffic from community to congregation *and* from congregation to community. For the people of God to be welcoming, they need to be equipped to be *with* the community (and not just in an event or gathering they are hosting). The Evangelist's eyes are observing both the congregation and community.

The gifts of the Prophet and Apostle leaders are to equip the congregation to participate in God's renewal work in the community. The liberating and sending environments they value are for the community as well as for the congregation. For the community to flourish, the congregation must be equipped to move into the neighborhood. While the Prophet leader's eyes are looking at the congregation from a distance and inviting them to where

God is already at work in the community, the Apostle leader's eyes are
looking within and beyond the community to discover where God is inviting the congregation to go next.

The position and perspective of
each APEST leader is important in
navigating sharing leadership. Sharing
APEST leadership will help shape the
structure of the church, allowing it to
function fully (see fig. 7.2).

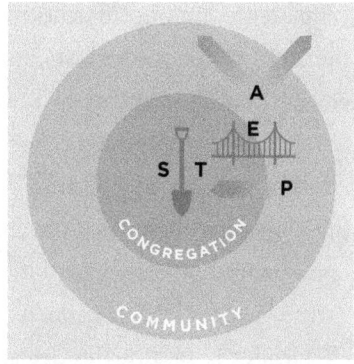

Figure 7.2. Equipping work of APEST

APEST AND SHARING LEADERSHIP: TIME

Equally important to the structure and positioning of the APEST leaders
is an understanding that each leader engages with time differently. Sharing
leadership will help shape the rhythm of the church so that APEST leaders
can work well together (see table 7.4).

The Teacher leader is more past oriented and is cautious in decision-
making, asking on behalf of the congregation, What is the truth? Because
this leader is deeply connected to the Word of God and the work of establishing a learning environment, content and accuracy are important. The
proverbial "what's beneath the glacier" is important work to excavate instead
of determining decisions and timing based on what's on the surface. Cautious excavating helps the congregation live sustainably and for the long haul.

The Shepherd leader is affected by the present, is informed by the past,
and is also cautious in decision-making, asking on behalf of the congregation, What is the danger? This leader's deep connection and love for the
True Shepherd determines the work of establishing a healing environment.
For this leader, guiding and guarding are important. In this environment
fences and boundaries aren't about being exclusive; they exist to wisely
protect what is valuable.

The Evangelist leader is present oriented and feels urgent in decision-
making because the main question to ask on behalf of the congregation is,

Who are we missing? Because of the leader's deep connection and love for the One who seeks the lost lamb, he or she is persistent in finding the lost coin and runs unashamedly toward the lost son in the work of establishing a welcoming environment. For this leader, the fast-paced and continuous effort of seeking and finding is important. Crossing that bridge between the congregation and community and making sure it's maintained, safe, and open keeps the congregation relevant to the community.

The Prophet leader is affected by the present and informed by the future. This leader is cautious in decision-making while asking on behalf of the congregation, What is the motivation? Because of the leader's deep connection and love for God's shalom and the work of establishing a liberating environment, the call to unveil the congregation's missional *why* is deep and meaningful work.

The Apostle leader is future oriented and is urgent in decision-making while asking on behalf of the congregation, What is the opportunity? This leader's deep connection and love for the King mirrors the kingdom that starts as small as a mustard seed but then grows to become the large, flourishing tree that provides for everyone and everything. The mature Apostle leader works to establish a sending environment; this hopeful vision moves the congregation into new kingdom opportunities, though at times they may be dead ends or risky.

Table 7.4. APEST and time

APEST	Time orientation	Timing capacity	Reasoning
Apostle	Future oriented	Urgent	What is the opportunity?
Prophet	Present-future oriented	Cautious	What is the motivation?
Evangelist	Present oriented	Urgent	Who are we missing?
Shepherd	Present-past oriented	Cautious	What is the danger?
Teacher	Past oriented	Cautious	What is the truth?

APEST AND SHARING LEADERSHIP: SEATS

Every summer, the beaches in Hawaii are teeming at sunrise with massive Hawaiian outrigger canoes. They say you don't paddle to get fit; you get fit to paddle. The short-distance races, stroke after stroke in concert, are mesmerizing to watch. The six paddlers must be in unison the whole time or risk capsizing and losing time in open ocean water. When Camille, who comes from generations of Hawaiian paddlers, first told me about the six-person canoe, she would always tell me her seat number. Seat one is the stroker and sets the pace for the canoe. Seat two keeps pace with the stroker but on the opposite side to keep balance. Seat three calls for stroke changes. Seats four and five are the power seats; they just drive the canoe forward. And seat six steers the canoe. The longer you're around paddling culture, the more you realize how quickly paddlers specialize in a preferred seat.

In my time working with church leaders, when utilizing APEST as a tool for sharing leadership, I have found it helpful to realize that a single mature leader often exhibits seat one, seat two, and seat three APEST leadership giftings (see fig. 7.3). Alan Hirsch writes, "We can have primary, secondary, and possibly tertiary ministries [APEST leadership giftings] all acting in a dynamic way. Each informs and qualifies the primary ministry [APEST leadership gifting] type."[3] There are two things to stress here: first, it's helpful for the leader to use APEST not as a personality test but as a tool; APEST guides the leader toward sharing leadership. Second, in thinking about these seats, it's helpful to keep in mind that the seats are pertinent for the mature leader, that is, a leader who is marked with humility, honor, hospitality, and hope.

Seat one, the primary APEST leadership gifting, is about what the leader values. Seat two, the secondary APEST leadership gifting, is the vehicle through which the value is expressed. I have come to find that seat three in a mature leader is the initial expression of immaturity under stress. Amy is one of the most humble, honoring, hospitable, and hopeful executive-level church leaders I know. I constantly joke with her that she will one day be the archbishop of Canterbury, and I'm only half joking. Amy leads so that both her church and her community are experiencing flourishing, and she will go from leading two churches to five in a year's time.

Amy and I both share seat one and seat two. We both are primarily Apostles, which means that we highly value cultivating sending environments, equipping the congregation to live out its calling for the sake of the community. We both are secondarily Prophets, which means that we value the vehicle of God's shalom in sending the people of God to experience their calling. We most often create equipping spaces where our people can discover their connectedness to God by experiencing God's shalom: renewal, liberation, and right relationship with others and with God.

The seat we differ in is in our seat three. Amy's tertiary seat is that of a Shepherd, and mine is that of an Evangelist. When Amy's leadership is under stress, as a mature Apostle-Prophet-Shepherd, she occasionally exhibits a protective bent, which allows insiders and outsiders to emerge. They may appear as a certain group of people to guide and guard and another group who are threats to guard against. When my leadership is under stress, as a mature Apostle-Prophet-Evangelist, my bent is to become entertaining and fun—not in a way that will necessarily connect people to one another but more in a way that avoids rejection. Mature leaders who utilize APEST as a helpful tool to participate in sharing leadership are often mindful of their seats. They know the values they champion (seat 1), use the vehicle through which they express their deep value (seat 2), and are mindful of their veiled immaturity when under stress (seat 3).

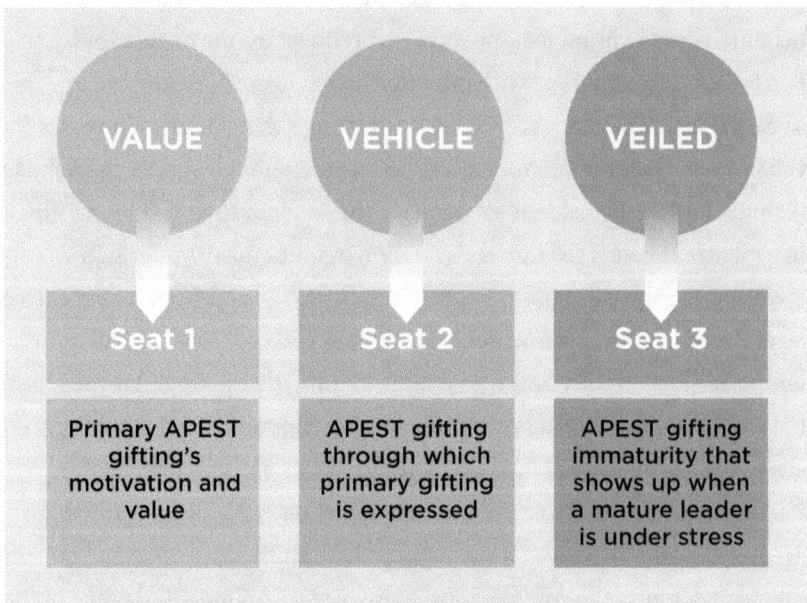

VALUE	VEHICLE	VEILED
Seat 1	Seat 2	Seat 3
Primary APEST gifting's motivation and value	APEST gifting through which primary gifting is expressed	APEST gifting immaturity that shows up when a mature leader is under stress

Figure 7.3. APEST and seats

So what happens when mature APEST leaders share leadership? In my local church, our Vision Team (executive leadership) is composed of five individuals, including myself. While I am an Apostle-Prophet-Evangelist, I'm so lucky to lead with Ed and Mark, who are mature Shepherd-Evangelist-Teachers. Meli who is a mature Prophet-Teacher-Shepherd, and Hanzo who is a mature Teacher-Prophet-Apostle. We share leadership by being clear about which APEST has first say in decisions.

- When we make decisions regarding people (relationships), the Shepherd and Evangelist voices are heard first because they are motivated by relationships—those on the inside and those on the outside.

- When we make decisions about content (truth), the Teacher and Prophet voices are heard first because they are motivated by integrity—accuracy and motivation.

- When we make decisions about mission, the Apostle and Prophet voices are heard first because they are motivated by the community—what's happening outside the church.

- When we make decisions about formation, the Teacher and Shepherd voices are heard first because they are motivated by the congregation—what's happening inside the church.

- When we make decisions regarding loss and grief, the Prophet and Shepherd voices are heard first because they are motivated by communal lament and care.

We also defer to one another with regard to timing. When the Apostle and Evangelist sense urgency, they discuss timing with the Prophet, Shepherd, and Teacher so that pacing for the congregation will be compassionate. When caution is sensed, timing is brought up to the Evangelist and Apostle so that pacing for the congregation won't be timid.

I have learned to mature as a leader by leading with Ed, Mark, Meli, and Hanzo. My fast pace as primarily an Apostle leader has grown to be patient and kind, my temptation to become resentful of the congregation has grown to be compassionate and understanding, and my sincere hope for experiencing God's kingdom here in Hawaii is more personally realized. I now experience a sending, liberating, welcoming, healing, and learning environment through our sharing leadership.

8

RECALLING APEST
FOR ALL TYPES OF
SHARING LEADERS

*We need to both appreciate and engage leaders and thinkers
who are involved in decolonial work, but it is not enough to let
them shoulder the burden on their own. Those who occupy a place
in centers of power must join in the anticolonial task of examining
institutional practices, challenging hurtful and oppressive structures,
and interrogating narratives of exclusion and superiority.*

RANDY WOODLEY

*Take away from me the noise of your songs;
to the melody of your harps I will not listen.
But let justice roll down like waters,
and righteousness like an ever-flowing stream.*

AMOS 5:23-24 ESV

WHEN WE DISCUSS APEST AND LEADERSHIP, and the goal of
sharing leadership, we must acknowledge the reality that the absence of
sharing leadership is not due to a lack of awareness or knowledge of APEST.
There is a severe deficit in sharing leadership in the church because dominant cultures in positions of power in the church have not shared it. While
in chapter nine I will navigate the different types of power and what kind
of power is necessary for sharing leadership, here I will pause to focus on
(1) how leadership in the church has excluded gender, race, and culture

and (2) how APEST has therefore excluded gender, race, and culture. We will close this chapter with some acknowledgment of how gender, race, and culture help to better form and inform us in sharing leadership through APEST.

LEADERSHIP AND GENDER

On June 14, 2023, a motion was passed by two-thirds vote at the Southern Baptist Convention (SBC) to include in Article III of its constitution a sixth criterion that defines a church's cooperation with the SBC as those that "affirm, appoint, or employ 'only men as any kind of pastor or elder as qualified by Scripture.'"[1] "Historically and culturally, the debate on women leadership in the church has almost nothing to do with a person's calling, skill sets and expertise, or spiritual and missional maturity."[2] In fact, *Christianity Today* published an article in June 2020 reviewing the many studies and surveys that show church attendees feel comfortable with "seeing women take on more prominent positions in the church."[3] At the time of this writing, the SBC, the largest Protestant denomination in the United States, maintained the decision to limit the role of pastor to only men. As a response to this, a secular academic, Frances Kneupper, wrote that our moment in 2023 is not that different from the moment in the late fourteenth century when spiritual women were also confronting the limits of leadership.

> Once again, authority is shifting and spiritual women are challenging the status quo. And once again, the male hierarchy of a major religious order is falling back on the same Bible verses to suppress this challenge. A similar unwillingness to share power seems to lie behind this decision. But the events of the late Middle Ages and Protestant Reformation provide a warning to the SBC. If the Convention—one of the most powerful forces in American religion—refuse to open its pulpits to women, the SBC may splinter, dramatically reducing its influence.[4]

I am a woman pastor, ordained in a denomination that, while started by a woman, has never had another woman in that top position again since 1923, over a hundred years ago. I was the first woman invited to be a part of the executive leadership team of an exciting local church plant in the fastest-growing and largest denomination in our area and the first woman to be a part of co-leadership without being married to my male co-lead counterparts. We grew from just twenty volunteers to 450 persons in the pews in just five years' time. And yet, I was asked to step down from my leadership position, not because of a lack of skill set or gifting, nor due to moral failure or absence of call from the church. Ultimately, I was asked to step down from leadership because I was a woman who was working with two men. At one point in my post, a person from human resources was brought in to have a conversation with me. She told me point blank that if I did not voluntarily step down from my leadership position, my husband would divorce me, he would change the locks on our house, and I would never see my children again. (Steve was never privy to this threat nor did the denomination ever invite him into a conversation.) At other times, I've witnessed congregants leave in the middle of service, and eventually the church, because they felt uncomfortable with a woman preacher. Still other times, I've been told by my congregants that it is a sin for women leaders to lead with men and have friendships with them.

Old Testament professor Carmen Joy Imes attends a church with a limited view of women pastoral leadership, and she reflects,

> As a woman trained in biblical studies with a lifetime of experience in ministry, I carry with me a longing for the full inclusion of women in every aspect of the church. For me, it's not a matter of equal rights but of faithfully responding to the call of God and the empowerment of the Spirit. No one has a right to the pulpit. Only those called by God and equipped to rightly handle the Word of God should be entrusted with the ministry of preaching. Those of us who sense this calling from God but are prevented from responding carry ongoing grief.[5]

While I have enduring hope that the way forward for the church is to share leadership, I am not without my own suffering amid paving a solid road for it in terms of leadership and gender.

LEADERSHIP AND RACE

While there are so many complexities related to church and race, particularly in the United States, the most prominent theme to address here is access to leadership. It would serve the church well to pay attention to contemporary society's conversation and push toward equity (rather than equality), which is mostly related to equitable access to resources. For leaders, resources include most importantly equipping, funding, and opportunities—as opposed to the popular belief that resources only pertain to basic needs of housing, food, education, and employment.[6] Equity in lieu of equality is also important to clearly delineate. Equity is about treating people justly, meaning adjusting to their historic, cultural, and socioeconomic circumstances. Equality is about giving everyone the same starting point. Leroy Barber writes about how minority leaders who work for mission organizations either funded by or led by White leaders, despite holding positions of titled power, possess neither power nor influence. "Funders, missions partners, and accountability colleagues may silently, even subconsciously, withdraw their support from leaders of color. . . . Frequently, they are not given backing, confidence or latitude to make mistakes."[7]

Alexia Salvatierra continues this discussion, particularly in how mainstream churches starkly contrast with the Base Ecclesial Communities (BEC),

> The privileged can be blind to the formation, opportunities, and connections that equipped them to succeed in a particular role, assuming that their capacity is inherent. Ironically, in the name of avoiding discrimination, they do not provide the necessary training or support for a marginalized leader to succeed. When they then fail, the original suspicion that they lacked the inherent capacity is reinforced. The person who fails may also carry that internalized societal perspective, and their sense of themselves as less inherently capable is also reinforced. For marginalized people to compete with privileged people, the playing field must be intentionally leveled, but this is so radically different from the way the world usually works.[8]

I am a BIPOC Christian leader. My first involvement at a national and international platform was with a White male-dominant church-planting organization. While I was excited for this opportunity, I learned quickly that my longing for growth in racial diversity within the organization was met with little backing and resources. My attempts at raising up more diverse leaders were met with an explanation that "lesser" leaders do not have the unconscious competency required to lead at this level. And my own request for funding and support was met with "we don't have the available resources now" while seeing my White leader counterparts get easier and faster access to those same resources. Ultimately, I exited the organization, after years of working to empower leaders below the executive team, increasing the racial and gender diversity of the participants, and being the only executive leader still leading in a local place. Even when my exit decision detailed reports of spiritual abuse and racial discrimination, it was met with silence, devoid of further investigation. While I have enduring hope that the way forward for the church is to share leadership, I am not without my own suffering while paving a solid road for it in terms of leadership and race.

LEADERSHIP AND CULTURE

When I talk about culture, I am not referring to a "process of individual enrichment"—"I am a cultured person"—or an activity aligned to an ascending trend—"I am with the culture."[9] Instead, I will focus on culture as the knowledge and behavior that characterizes a particular group of people—"I am of a culture."[10] Culture, H. Richard Niebuhr suggested, should be understood as "the 'artificial, secondary environment' which man superimposes on the nature. It comprises language, habits, ideas, beliefs, customs, social organization, inherited artifacts, technical processes, and values."[11] Peter Smith and Michael Bond have written,

> Valid understanding of the relationship between cultures and persons requires an adequate conceptualization of the many contexts within which individuals work and live. These contexts include the more

distal features of the individual's birth ecology and ethno-national group history. These features converge more proximally upon individual experience as "process" variables, through the institutional-normative constraints and affordances encountered through socialization into a diverse set of cultural groupings. This enculturation is then revealed in the individual's response profile of values, beliefs, choices, and behaviors at any given time.[12]

Culture, or what is deemed as normal or right, often lacks flexibility but becomes a reference point, often determined by a dominant or the most power-positioned culture. The church and church leadership do not escape this. Leadership must recognize that the culture in the church and therefore leadership culture in the church, should be set by Christ, not by a dominant human culture. In addition, church culture in the West must include immigrant church culture since it is the fastest-growing culture today. Robert Chao Romero writes,

> In the decades to come, immigrants and immigrant families will fuel the numerical growth of the US church, as well as the US in general. The data clearly show that the white US population is aging and having fewer children. Immigration will sustain the US socially, economically, and even spiritually. These domestic trends coincide with the fact that the global pendulum of Christianity has already swung in the direction of Africa, Latin America, and Asia. The expression that Christianity is a "white man's religion" is already not true. The present and future face of the Church of Jesus of Nazareth is "brown," and Christianity is returning to its historical origins as a faith of the marginalized born in the Near East. In the decades to come, Christian immigrants from Latin America, Africa, and Asia will redefine the US church in practice, polity, and theology.[13]

I am a first-generation Korean American who immigrated to Philadelphia with my family, my parents, and my three older brothers during the third round of immigration in the post–Korean War era. At that time, the quota system of the United States' 1965 Immigration and Naturalization

Act was revoked in order to welcome experts and professionals from East Asia.[14] I have my fair share of traumatic stories from my youth and adulthood with dominant-cultured people asking incessantly where I come from, if I can speak English, how I can see through slitted eyes, and where my national allegiance lies. I have experienced the objectification and exoticism of Asian women in professional settings, including in the church.[15] I currently pastor a church in Honolulu, Hawaii, where stories of immigration as heritage are still told today. I write in "Assimilation Displaces, and the Church Is Complicit,"

> It is not lost on me that my Korean American story has such a keen affinity to my beloved Hawaiian community's story. It is not lost on me that both of our long-lined and heritage-rich families have endured occupation, loss of language and cultural identity, and a participation as the *"other."* . . . I often wonder what the American (and perhaps the extended Western) Church can learn from the stories of Asian Americans, Native Hawaiians, and Pacific Islanders (AANHPI), whose stories are not separate from the Church but are a part of the history of the American story. There are so many intersections between the history of the Church and history of colonization. The Church implemented colonization in order to displace a people group's culture, language, and identity. The Church practiced colonialism in order to demand the assimilation of so many cultures, including AANHPI's, voices, reflections, ideas, and values. . . .
>
> The Church often squeezes the Kingdom of God to become assimilated to its own image: to its own worship style, language, and preferences. It's a dominant cultural decision, whether subconscious or intentional. In the history of the Church's colonial ambitions, assimilation to the empowered and dominant culture of the White Church was often the end goal. But the depiction of the Kingdom of God throughout the Scriptures is one of keeping cultures, language, and identities intact *as they are.* This is the brilliance of the multitude worshiping the Lamb together in John's vision—every culture,

language, and people group stood before the throne of the Lamb as their fully human self, cultural identity fully engaged.[16]

While I have enduring hope that the way forward for the church is to share leadership, I am not without my own suffering while paving a solid road for it in terms of leadership and culture.

THE GIFT OF LEADERSHIP THROUGH GENDER, RACE, AND CULTURE

While the following will be in no way a complete list of contributions that women, BIPOC, and immigrants have made in sharing leadership, I will highlight a few key points. Women, in both church and secular arenas (most effectively in business and education), have championed the value of collaboration, conversation, and hospitality more than their male counterparts have. God is committed to a leadership that equips the people of God for works of service that contribute to unity and Christlikeness for the benefit of the larger community around us. Inspired by this principle, women in leadership have contended for both women and men to be a part of the image bearers of God (Gen 1:26-27) in participating in and partnering with God in the renewal of all things. Kate Coleman, the first Black woman to be an accredited Baptist minister in the UK Baptist Union, comments,

> In our era, the most successful women leaders appear to be both competent and warm, tough and compassionate, assertive yet morally and emotionally responsible, and decisive and creative; and they are liked as well as respected. Women tend to have greater influence when they blend their leadership style to incorporate these masculine and feminine characteristics. This is a challenging goal for any woman in leadership but one that many women strive to achieve. Until the idea of leadership is both male and female, women in leadership may be prone to greater misunderstanding, resistance, and opposition and even greater conflict than that faced by their male counterparts.[17]

Among BIPOC leaders, particularly in the Base Ecclesial Communities and "hush harbors" (historically, secluded meeting places for enslaved people), launch points of the Latino and Black churches, we see the leadership value of intimacy, meeting the community's real needs, and advocating politically and socially for equity. In alignment with the kind of leadership God desires, BIPOC leadership has contended most for the social, political, and justice-oriented common good. As Alexia Salvatierra concludes, "The BEC movement arose at a particular point in time in the history of the Catholic Church and in the broader society in Latin America and the Philippines. BECs represented an unprecedented level of engagement by poor and marginalized people as protagonists in their common spiritual and social lives." She adds,

> While scholars have questioned whether BECs were fully representative of the poor and truly integrated spiritual and social dimensions, powerful evidence suggests they did create a new model of being church that has potential relevance for anyone seeking to integrate personal spiritual formation, communal care, power-sharing, and social transformation under the leadership of marginalized and oppressed people. As we seek to draw inspiration and guidance from this movement for Christian community today, we will build on the core BEC principles of the preferential option for the poor, the building of the family of God, and the mission of becoming the soul and leaven of the society.[18]

And finally, the fast-growing immigrant churches, particularly in the United States, have contributed innovation and the honoring of diverse reflections of the multicultural people of God. In alignment with the kind of leadership God favors, immigrant church leadership has contended against the dominant culture's propensity for assimilation of "other" cultures. The immigrant church is at the forefront of reflecting a fuller version of the corporate image bearer that John envisioned, "After this I looked, and there before me was a great multitude that no one could count, from every nation, tribe, people and language, standing before the throne and before the Lamb" (Rev 7:9). Richard J. Mouw observes,

One of the more fascinating proposals that have been made in theological discussions of the biblical notion of "the image of God" is that this image has a "corporate" dimension. That is, there is no one human individual or group who can fully bear or manifest all that is involved in the image of God, so that there is a sense in which that image is collectively possessed. The image of God is, as it were, parceled out among the peoples of the earth. By looking at different individuals and groups we get glimpses of different aspects of the full image of God.[19]

In light of these reflections and as I continue to do meaningful locally rooted and translocal ministry work among shared gender leadership, I feel such a sense of hope. BIPOC-specific leadership spaces, including the immigrant churches, present a hopeful vision for the present and future church. I am a woman-BIPOC-immigrant leader in the church. Amid the pain and hardship of pioneering work, though undoubtedly on the coattails of so many before me, I feel more committed to sharing leadership than ever before.

APEST AND WOMEN, BIPOC, AND IMMIGRANT CHURCH LEADERSHIP

As I've shared before, knowledge of the intricacies of APEST is a powerful tool in developing sharing leadership. As each APEST leader becomes a self-regulating center of influence in how the people of God are equipped to mature into the likeness of Christ, sharing leadership leads the congregation to be fully equipped for the mission of Christ—to be connected to the community. Within the complex narrative of sharing leadership among gender, race, and culture, we also find the beauty of learning and experiencing APEST in these spaces.

Under the quintessential "white gaze,"[20] the dominant Western church has a veiled conception of what APEST and sharing leadership look like. Jonathan Tran observes, "Just as race narrows what counts as suffering, so it narrows pathways for shared forms of life."[21] I would extend that thought:

the dominant White evangelical church narrows what counts as gender-based, racial, and cultural suffering and success, and so it narrows pathways for sharing leadership.

I know Apostle Latina leaders who could outpace everyone of us. However, because of their commitment to be identified *with* each of their disadvantaged communities, they have taken disadvantaged leadership positions (with the lowest-paying jobs) and refuse to create environments of competition (even though they could win and experience more material success). There's just too much at stake to abandon these congregations that are already starting from a loss. These Latina leaders are often misappropriated as Prophet leaders, but it's their racial heritage that demands that the church experience their calling to the most disadvantaged in the community.

I know Apostle Black male leaders who have inherited their congregation from their Teacher-gifted fathers. These men would excel entrepreneurially outside the church (and have a lot more financial security), but they are committed to staying with their Black congregants so they can encourage them to participate in tangible flourishing with the community (and not just tangible flourishing for themselves).

I know Apostle immigrant Vietnamese male leaders who all share the story of arriving as refugees on boats. They could be the most innovative and lucrative business people. Instead, they commit to a bilingual congregation, seen perpetually as outsiders, in order to inspire them to live out their innovative spirits for the benefit of their community. All these leaders, I would argue, are better poised to sharing leadership than many of their White counterparts.

If we as leaders don't begin to include and be flexible, particularly in the languages, stories, and leaders we elevate in our meditation of Ephesians 4, then we will miss out on the gift of women, BIPOC, and immigrant church leadership voices. These voices are needed in our present culture as we move into the future church. Without these voices, the future church will be devoid of diversity, robust equipping of the people of God, and full reflection of the Son of God.

Traditionally, APEST vocabulary around these leadership giftings felt more nuanced toward men or expected women to lead like men. Apostle Leaders are male church leaders who are entrepreneurial, whereas the Apostolic leader description most used for women is that of a midwife—the one who helps others birth something new. Instead of standing behind a pulpit, Indigenous leaders lead congregations who gather around a circle, where the Teacher leader best exercises a mature learning environment rather than an immature teaching environment. The Black church, particularly in the civil rights movement of the 1960s and the more recent Black Lives Matter protests, has been at the frontlines demonstrating what the Prophet leader does best—establish an environment for liberation that is not devoid of faith. The immigrant church, particularly the Latina/o church, has stalwartly provided a place of welcome, as the mature Evangelist leader, especially for those who have been the least welcomed in society.

I have enduring hope that the way forward for the church is to share leadership.

PART THREE

SHARING

LEADERSHIP

IN REAL LIFE

They may have asked for the Holy Spirit to come, but they did not ask for this. This is real grace, untamed grace. It is the grace that replaces our fantasies of power over people with God's fantasy for desire for people.

WILLIE JAMES JENNINGS

9

THE POWER OF SHARING LEADERSHIP

Identarianism's individualizing approach will not do. If we hope to succeed, we will need others.

JONATHAN TRAN

But God has put the body together . . . so that there should be no division in the body, but that its parts should have equal concern for each other. If one part suffers, every part suffers with it; if one part is honored, every part rejoices with it.

1 CORINTHIANS 12:24-26

"WHY DON'T WE JUST GET ALL THE LEADERS TOGETHER and have a conversation about decentralizing our organization? It sounds super exciting, and I'm sure they'd love to hear and contribute to the conversation!" As one of the three executive team members, I was excited about inviting the second-tier leaders, most of whom had been a part of this international training organization longer than I had and were all currently leading in their own locally rooted ministries. We were at the point of choosing how our organization would grow. As an Apostle leader myself, it felt like meaningful work. After a decade of existing as a training organization, we were finally poised to think about how to connect our alumni church communities into tightly knit communities for the sake of their cities or regions. We could open the leadership platform so the community could also learn from one another and from our best practices and worst mistakes. It felt like what I've always dreamed of—to be a part of an organization that thought about how to raise the tide for all ships. And here was an opportunity to tap into the wealth of leadership resources in these extremely mature, experienced, and practitioner-based leaders.

But Jonah did not agree. "No, no, I think it's better to just do one-on-one conversations."

"What?!" I replied puzzled, "No, if you just do one-on-ones, then we'd lose the gift of hearing from one another and learning from one another. Some folks may be able to better articulate things; others are probably better at thinking of real-life models. These leaders want to contribute." I paused for a moment, having worked closely with him for some time now. Changing my tone, I considered, "Hmmm . . . I can hear some hesitation in your voice. I wonder what you might be guarding."

He replied, "I'd prefer one-on-one conversations so that I don't lose control of the room."

Because of Jonah's fear of losing control, this organization never tapped into the wealth of leaders who had stood by his side for almost a decade. Sadly, today nearly all those leaders have transitioned from under his executive leadership. They never had a platform to make contributions, and the organization remains a training organization that favors White male leadership.

I remember when one staff member in this organization was transitioning out. Lori had started with the team from the very beginning, the only Black person on staff for a decade. She led and organized countless conferences and conversations on behalf of this organization, but in the end the lack of clarity and unwillingness to share power prompted her departure. The executive team made no public acknowledgment of her leaving. My heart shattered for her. As a junior member of the executive team, I didn't really know what to do. However, I did ask all the second-tier leaders to send a note, a prayer, or a word of encouragement or thanks. I printed each of those words, rolled them up, and tied them with a piece of raffia, which we use in Hawaii to make *lei poʻo* or crown lei. I received my first *lei poʻo*, given on special occasions, at my ordination. I make them for my daughters' school promotions, and I gave one to my mom on her seventieth birthday.

I collected those words, tied by raffia, and included a local artist's painting of a beautiful *puakenikeni lei*. I wrote to Lori, "This is so small in comparison to the way you ought to have been honored. But we honor you and are so grateful for your leadership all these years." A few weeks later, after all the transition had happened, she thanked me for the gift and said, "Your caliber of leadership shows in how you treat us."

Sharing leadership is actually about sharing power. If we as leaders don't know how to do this, then we can label our churches and organizations "sharing leadership" all we want, but in the end we are just holding onto power while using and abusing others.

SHARING LEADERSHIP AND POWER

Sharing leadership in the church is one of the most powerful and effective ways to equip the people of God for the sacred unity and communal Christlike maturity to foster a flourishing church that connects to community. Before we discuss how to identify leaders capable of sustaining the structure of organizations in sharing leadership, we will look at why sharing leadership is so powerful and effective. The key is to understand how this framework for leadership relates to power. It's important to highlight how power works in sharing leadership, how power is given up willingly in sharing leadership, how power is exchanged mutually in sharing leadership, and how the lasting fruit of sharing leadership is in its gift of empowering more leaders. The impact on the leader is invaluable.

In the act of willingly giving up power, leaders experience the gift of *kenōsis* (self-emptying). The kenotic journey of experiencing descent and humility, relinquishing power, becoming de-centered, and following the selfless way of Christ, cultivates in leaders the gift of a deeper discipleship—denying themselves, taking up their cross daily, and imitating Jesus (Mk 8:34). The act of mutually exchanging power in sharing leadership invites leaders to regularly practice detaching from the temptation of grabbing and holding on to power. This regular practice cultivates in leaders a release from selfishly motivated desire for power through control, crowd, and contribution. Instead, the ability to command control, mobilize a crowd, and make meaningful contributions isn't used to wield power but is mutually shared among a set of leaders who are equipping the people of God. And finally, the act of freely giving away power and empowering more leaders impacts a single leader by cultivating hope in prayer to the Lord of the harvest for more workers (Lk 10:2).[1] When leaders practice seeing the potential of leadership in others, using clear marks of maturity (of humility, hospitality, honor, and hope), there is a deep sense of joy that they are not alone in the work.[2]

But sharing leadership doesn't end with its impact on just the leader. There is a profound impact on the congregation and for the surrounding community. When leaders willingly give up power, the congregation welcomes *kenōsis* as a normalized way of imitating Jesus. It will generate a gathering of people who won't resist a kenotic journey but expect it for their own connection with Christ. When leaders mutually exchange power, the congregation begins to value unity and maturity over proximity to power. A congregation with proximity to power (in this case, the leader) may succumb to feeling either safe or special (chap. 2).

But, when a congregation witnesses the regular practice of power being mutually exchanged among a set of diverse leaders, they experience the peace (instead of just the desire to feel safe) that comes through unity and Christlike identity/maturity (instead of just the desire to feel special). Their dependence lead them to seek proximity to the leader; their longing will be to have proximity to Christ. And finally, when leaders freely give away power, the congregation is invited into joining in the work of God. Their expectation on the leader isn't to be entertained, nurtured, or fed; their expectation on the leader is to be equipped for the works of service for the flourishing and benefit of the community around them.

SHARING LEADERSHIP GIVES UP POWER

In *Reckoning with Power*, David Fitch helpfully categorizes power according to four dynamics.[3]

1. Power *over*
2. Power *within*
3. Power *to*
4. Power *through*

I will introduce an addition to these dynamics: power *with*. In the practice of giving up power, sharing leadership does not abdicate power. On the contrary, by sharing, leaders engage in relinquishing power in order to consistently establish power *with* (see table 9.1).

Table 9.1. A congregation's potential response to proximity to power

Power type	
Power OVER	Dominance
Power THROUGH	Influence
Power WITHIN	Systemic
Power TO	Replacement
Power WITH	Partnership

Power is present in almost all social situations we find ourselves in. Whether it be the corporation you work at, the village zoning committee, the street crew you work on, the neighborhood, the playgrounds, the sports organizations, the local schools, or that charitable organization you volunteer at, power is at work. In all these places, persons have stakes in what is going on. Each organization gathers a people for a purpose. And power is what moves us and what gets things done. Power is also at work in your local church.[4]

As discussed in chapter two, power *over* refers to dominant power—held by those who are able to have enforceable authority over others. Power *through* refers to dynamic power—held by those who are able to have enforceable influence over others. Power *within* refers to a cultural response moving away from overt dominance to an accepted systemic and en-forceable set of underlying rules, systems, ethics, or cultures. Power *to* refers to those to whom power is given and is now newly enforced; it is tied closely to empowering a new set of people in order to override an old system.[5]

Iris Marion Young states, in challenging the current prevailing view of social justice giving way to distributive justice, that "bringing power under the logic of distribution" only misrepresents what power is, as if it is "a kind of stuff posted by individual agents in greater or lesser amounts." She continues, saying that power is "a relation rather than a thing."[6] In line with this thought that power is more a relationship than a possession, each of the four dynamic ways we relate to power does not allow power to be fully shared. Not really. Each has the opportunity to manipulate, abuse, withhold, and limit power (see chapter two, table 2.3).

The infamous Mars Hill megachurch empire built by its founding pastor, Mark Driscoll, is a stark example of a local church community experiencing leadership via power *over*. His Calvinistic theology of God's infallible sovereignty "easily slipped into a movement centered around *his own* sovereignty," leading to the church finally formally charging him with being arrogant, quick-tempered, harsh in speech, and domineering in his leadership.[7]

The centuries-old Anglican churches in the United Kingdom are riddled with struggles over power *within*, or systemic power, because emerging leaders are required to follow an aged tradition to achieve ordination. In speaking with one of its executive leaders, Timothy could tell how pressing it was to consider change in order to empower both emerging leaders and BIPOC leaders in its painfully colonial and White approach to leadership. But such change might take centuries to implement within its existing rules, systems, ethics, and culture.

Marques shared about coming to faith in his Southern Black church, where the culture and racial heritage allowed him to feel comfortable in his own skin: Black preachers, Black gospel worship, Black congregants. But he eventually moved his young family out of the church because, despite cultural comfort, the leadership was dealing with power *to*, or replacement of power. The power dynamics, although not White, were controlled by older Black male leaders who wanted to hold onto the power they had so desperately fought for.

Cornerstone Church in California, founded by Francis Chan, grew from thirty congregants to six thousand in just fifteen years. But then in 2010, at the peak of his fame, Chan announced his resignation. Cornerstone was wrestling with the dynamic of power *through*, or the leader's influence. In an interview Chan shared, "One of the problems at our church is when I hear the words 'Francis Chan' more than I hear the words 'Holy Spirit.'"[8]

Before offering my contribution that sharing leadership entails power *with*, I will interject here that the concept of power within the Scriptures is also closely enmeshed with not just human power but with the powers that Jesus often mentioned (Lk 10:19). N. T. Wright writes of the powers,

> A new sort of power will be let loose upon the world, and it will be the power of self-giving love. This is the heart of the revolution that was launched on Good Friday. You cannot defeat the usual sort of power by the usual sort of means. If one force overcomes another, it is still "force" that wins. Rather, at the heart of the victory of God over all the powers of the world there lies self-giving love, which, in obedience to the ancient prophetic vocation, will give its life "as a ransom for many." Exactly as in Isaiah 53, to which that phrase alludes, the death of the one on behalf of the many will be the key by which the powers are overthrown, the kingdom of God ushered in (with the glorious divine Presence seen in plain sight by the watchmen on Jerusalem's walls), the covenant renewed, and creation itself restored to its original purpose.[9]

For ancient readers, the Scriptures were describing powers that pertain to human, spiritual, and systemic representations.

Sharing leadership gives up power by participating in power *with*. It continues Young's thought that power is not a possession but a relationship, and sharing power means to hold and exercise power alongside others. It's the sharing of power *with* others that "moves us and gets things done."[10] Sharing leadership doesn't abdicate power or abuse it; it participates alongside others to communally relate to power. Sharing leadership imitates Jesus, who constantly models self-giving love as the way to give up power in order to work alongside others. God also establishes power *with* by inviting his creation, his image bearers, to participate alongside him in his good work (Gen 1:26-28). Sharing leadership involves giving up power, that is, the kind of power that relates to others insufficiently (or violently) through dominance (power *over*), influence (power *through*), systems (power *within*), or replacement (power *to*). Sharing leadership gives up these kinds of power in order to take up power *with*—partnership (see table 9.1).

SHARING LEADERSHIP EXCHANGES POWER

In order to think practically about how power is exchanged in sharing leadership, we'll turn to already existing models of sharing leadership outside the church. Sharing leadership or "polycentric leadership" is a concept borrowed heavily from organizational structuring in business and political fields, as evidenced in the 2020 OCMS Montagu Barker Lecture Series: "Polycentric Theology, Mission and Mission Leadership"[11] and is defined by Kirk Franklin in his thesis as

> the concept of allowing for self-regulating centers of influence within a singular structure. This occurs when there are many centers of power or importance within a political, cultural or socio-economic system. The multiple centers may be of leadership, power, authority, ideology, or importance within a larger boundary or structure.[12]

One key concept to mutually exchanging power is that of self-regulating centers of influence. This is where APEST as a tool for sharing leadership is pivotal. Based on the APEST giftings to equip the people of God, each of the APEST giftings can be seen as a "self-regulating center of influence" (see fig. 9.1).

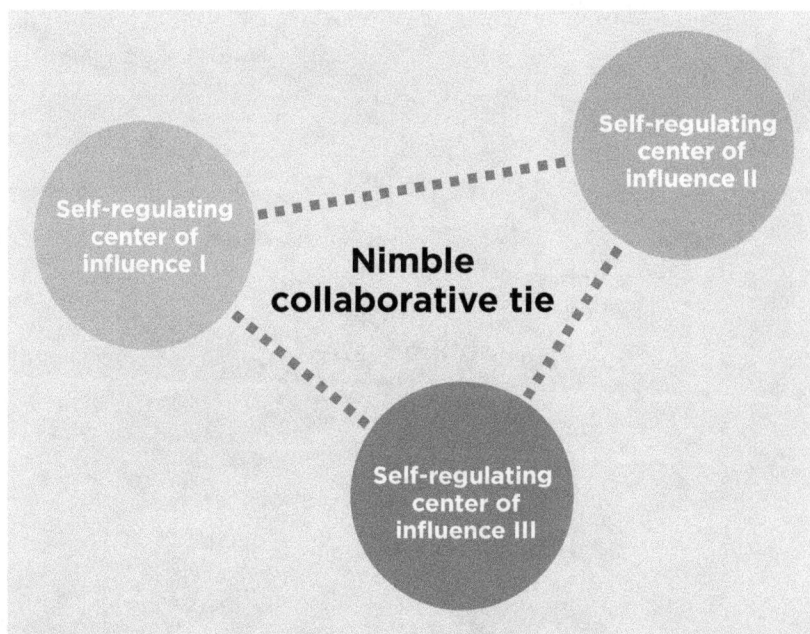

Figure 9.1. Self-regulating centers of influence

As self-regulating centers of influence, the APEST leaders remain connected to one another through a nimble collaborative tie (see fig. 9.2). The thriving environment of the Apostle is collaboratively tied to the healing environment of the Shepherd. The learning environment of the Teacher is collaboratively tied to the liberating environment of the Prophet, as is the welcoming environment of the Evangelist. The gift of a nimble collaborative tie generates allowances for both innovation and trustworthiness—both new and traditioned.

Nora Hamzel writes,

Research findings point to a new phase in leadership practice that highlights women's participation as contributing to trusting and safe environments that nurture collaboration creating new cultures that allow for deep learning. These findings strongly are connected with distributed leadership . . . that highlights distributed leadership as a collaborate activity.[13]

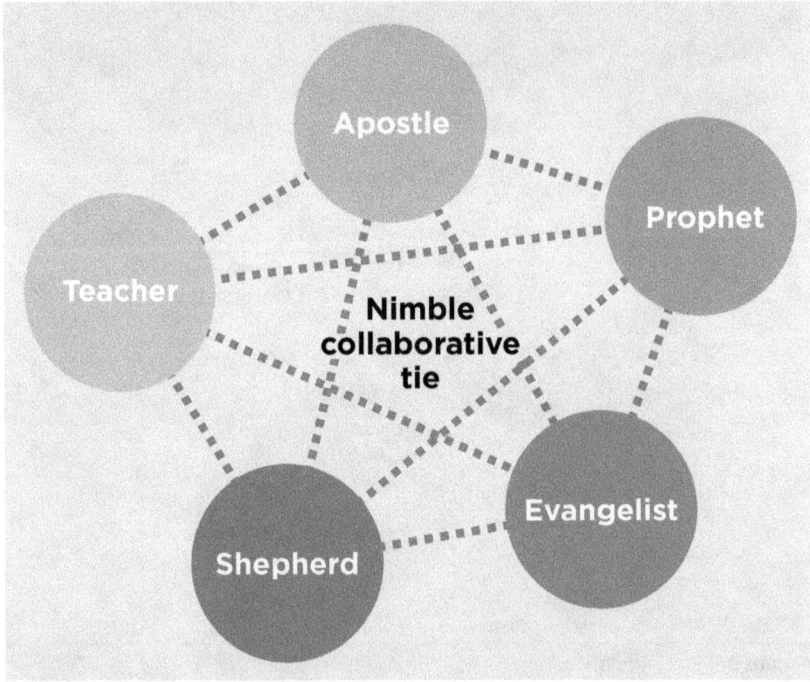

Figure 9.2. APEST as self-regulating centers of influence

Additionally, Deborah Ancona defines distributed leadership, or nimble leadership, as "collaborative, autonomous practices managed by a network of formal and informal leaders across an organization."[14]

The key concept to mutually exchanging power is that a nimble or collaborative leadership relationship ties the self-regulating centers of influences together. This kind of connection entails high relational trust, clear Spacing seems a bit tight, practiced fidelity and reliability, and each of the mature leaders understanding one another's self-regulating centers of influence, their values and goals.

Distributed leadership that practically utilizes self-regulating centers of influence in management is becoming the growing antidote to the emerging culture's great resignation. It not only gives permission to contribute the best expertise, knowledge, skills, and ideas. It also fuels commitment through both innovation and collaboration by shifting leadership questions from Who's to blame for this failure, and how do we fix it? to What did we learn, and how can we improve?[15]

A final key concept is that the practice of mutually exchanging power allows the leaders to ask questions that help to cultivate more sharing leadership. It moves the leaders from asking accusatory noncollaborative questions to collaborative questions: How can we move forward? There's an expectation that we won't nail it every time, but each effort is an opportunity to learn and grow from our mistakes and missteps.

SHARING LEADERSHIP EMPOWERS MORE LEADERS

Importantly, the significant act of freely giving away power and empowering more leaders impacts the leader by cultivating a hope to pray to the Lord of the harvest for more workers (Lk 10:2). In having the kind of outlook in which leaders practice seeing the potential of leadership in others, using clear marks of maturity (of humility, hospitality, honor, and hope), there is a deep sense of joy that convinces leaders that they are not alone in the work.

The beauty of sharing leadership is that leaders freely give power away without abdicating it. They answer Jesus' call to join him in the work of both *kenōsis* and flourishing. They also mutually exchange power repeatedly through collaboration and high relational trust. As a result, leaders begin to see the world as Jesus sees it:

> After this the Lord appointed seventy-two others and sent them two by two ahead of him to every town and place where he was about to go. He told them, "The harvest is plentiful, but the workers are few. Ask the Lord of the harvest, therefore, to send out workers into his harvest field." (Lk 10:1-2)

Sharing leadership allows the leader to partner with Jesus and see that the harvest is indeed plentiful and longs with him for increased partners in the work.

Sharing leadership cultivates a hope and a vision for an increase of those who will partner with Christ; they are not treated as competition or incompetent. And when leadership multiplies through hope and potential, then the congregation is constantly invited into the joyful work of God.

They are no longer spectators but participants—partners, in fact, equipped for the works of service for the flourishing and benefit of the community around them. Spectators expect to be served; partners expect to serve. Competitors fear loss and being replaced; partners expect more people to join in. Those who need to be "fed" hold commitment loosely; partners have skin in the game and are deeply engaged.

I prayed for nearly fifteen years that God would provide indigenous Hawaiian workers to be a part of the harvest work. I've had countless conversations with other senior pastors about why local churches lacked local leaders. Most of the fastest-growing church plants had primarily Asian American or mainland transplants as leaders but no indigenous Hawaiian leaders. Those with Hawaiian leaders were in tiny invisible pockets or old declining churches. One senior pastor, a White American from the West Coast, confided that local men were lazy. "They're not motivated. I've tried. The best they can do is be a part of the setup and breakdown crew." Now, mind you, first, I asked in general about local leadership, not male leadership; this leader did not hesitate to exclude women for consideration for leadership. Second, I asked in what ways he tried, and he replied that they posted notices during the service announcements but got no responses.

I did not think that there were so few local Indigenous church leaders in Hawaii because the culture was lazy; I believed there were so few local leaders because we did not ask.[16]

When Craig and Roz said yes to being leaders in our local church, I went home that day and cried. They are both middle-aged lovers of Jesus with Hawaiian roots, who love their large family and their community and have discipled and shepherded countless local indigenous Hawaiian men and women. I couldn't believe that they were saying yes to being a part of our pioneering church.

I asked, "What made you say yes?" I remember Craig's response. He's the kind of guy who is both a "guy's guy" but is soft spoken. He often mumbles something pretty witty under his breath, but you may be lucky enough to catch it. He loves his powerhouse prophetic wife and has the fiercest compassion for her. He serves others without ever being asked and is slow to speak and slow to anger. He doesn't say much, but when he does, everybody in our community leans in a bit more and pays attention. He simply answered, "Well, Eun, because you asked. Nobody asked me before."

SHARING LEADERSHIP PARTNERS
WITH THE COMMUNITY

When sharing leadership moves from new to normal, it also recognizes that power must be shared *with* the community it longs to serve. When power is utilized *with*, then the church must always consider the community's voice at the table. The Community Engagement Program of the Johns Hopkins Institute for Clinical and Translational Research conducted a study that partnered researchers and community partners to evaluate and discuss community involvement in health research. Three key themes were identified: (1) community engagement is an ongoing and iterative process, (2) community partner roles must be well-defined and clearly communicated, and (3) mutual trust and transparency are central to community engagement.[17] Community-development work must involve community engagement; the church's relationship with the community is no different from those with healthcare.

In our local church, we have experienced many times over how community engagement is iterative: We've held "Listening Campaigns"[18] to hear from local community leaders in agriculture (land issue is social justice in Hawaii), small-business owners, and local artists. We've joined with the community as they hosted us, for example, to help our local Food Bank, partner with our local Big Brothers Big Sisters program, participate in beach clean-ups and park clean-ups, or host a Pa'ina Keokeo dinner for the small-business owners who were the first to invest in the neighborhood. The work is not intended to merely check a box for community service. It's an active way for our leaders to keep an ongoing seat at the table for the community.

Sharing leadership gives up other kinds of powers in order to hold on to power *with*. Sharing leadership practices the mutual exchange of power through self-regulating centers of influence actively participating in nimble collaborative ties. Sharing leadership not only opens a better path for empowering more leaders, but it also engenders vital connections with the community.

10

HOW TO START
SHARING LEADERSHIP

*A leader sees greatness in other people. He nor she can
be much of a leader if all she sees is herself.*

MAYA ANGELOU

*The next day Jesus decided to leave for Galilee.
Finding Philip, he said to him, "Follow me."
Philip, like Andrew and Peter, was from the town of Bethsaida.
Philip found Nathanael and told him, "We have found the one
Moses wrote about in the Law, and about whom the prophets
also wrote—Jesus of Nazareth, the son of Joseph."
"Nazareth! Can anything good come from there?" Nathanael asked.
"Come and see," said Philip.*

JOHN 1:43-46

THE VERY FIRST GATHERING with our brand-new church plant was
at a beautiful old Hawaiian home next to a canal that fed into the Pacific
Ocean. Picture freshly clipped birds-of-paradise set amid bright green
monstera leaves, the shine of carved koa wood furniture, and fresh trade
winds blowing through the indoor/outdoor living space. We broke freshly
made bread and popped open a bottle of wine to take Communion together. Women and men, young and old, blue-collar and white-collar,

Indigenous, local, and transplants alike, Filipino, Japanese, Brazilian, Chinese, Korean, Hawaiian, Samoan, and White, sat at table together.

Amanda in particular was very nervous about gathering for the first time, making sure to stay at the edge of the group. She confessed she felt out of place, didn't know anyone, and was unsure of her fit. Grabbing her shoulders gently but squarely and looking into her eyes, I reassured her, "Amanda, just try. Nobody here actually knows each other that well. Everyone is equally unsure of how they fit in, but we're all gonna try and see how this works."

After taking Communion while the sun was setting on the ocean, we could feel the sense of purpose drawing everyone together. *Fresh* was the appropriate word to describe this moment. Fresh eyes, fresh bread, fresh wine, fresh air, fresh vision, and fresh community. I shared with this new crew of Jesus followers, numbering twenty altogether, about Jesus banking his entire life, death, and resurrection on how we will treat one another. That, more than anything else we will become or do, tells our neighbors here in Hawaii and the rest of the world who Jesus is. Jesus banked his entire ministry on his followers having sincere and self-giving love for one another.

We then dove a little into APEST and tried our hand at dividing up the room into Apostles, Prophets, Evangelists, Shepherds, and Teachers in different corners. Most had soft nervous giggles. Some were uncertain about their choices, and others calmly but confidently walked over to their spot. There was a group of reserved Teachers who took the back by the dock. The social-in-different-ways Shepherds and Evangelists looked at one another across the room feeling affirmed in their growing numbers. A couple of Prophets were still unsure about their location and were not making eye contact. And I, by the kitchen, was the lone Apostle. The origin story of our local church was that of equally numbered Shepherds and Evangelists and a smattering of Teachers. There were very few self-identified Prophets and one Apostle. Our church launch team was extremely skewed (see fig. 10.1).

In this chapter, I'll use my local community as an example to show the process of identifying leaders who want to share leadership. And I'll offer recommendations on how to identify and invite people into shared leadership that instills a culture of empowering leaders who share power.

IDENTIFYING SHARING LEADERS

As Christine Pohl reminds us, "Human beings were made for living in community, and it is in community that we flourish and become most fully human."[1] One of the discipleship core essentials in our church is "thick community," by which we mean every disciple commits to the value of "I belong to God's unified, growing, and diverse family."[2] Thick community is necessary in the moments when we experience tension and a desire to move in opposite directions from each other. Just as the thickness of a rope matters in a game of tug of war, so does the thickness of a community matter. This is not so true in times of peace when we're already moving toward one another, but we experience it in times of conflict when we want to pull away from one another. A piece of thread will not endure even one tug before it snaps in half while a thick, braided rope will survive despite strong forces pulling in opposite directions.

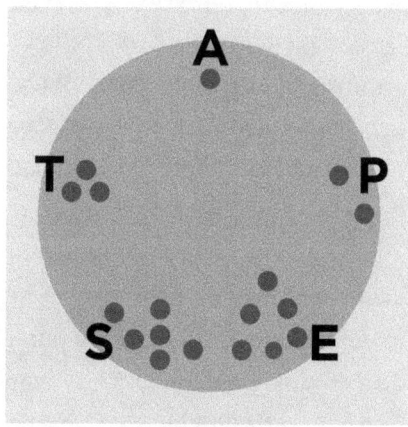

Figure 10.1. APEST skew

The two tools we used to equip every Jesus follower in our local church in thick community revolved around conflict resolution and differing preferences. For the first six months of our origin story, we only focused on these two principles: being a thick over thin community and APEST. Before any public gathering as a Jesus community, before any act of service or ministry, before any delineation of leadership, we focused on how to love and work with one another through our anticipated differences and preferences.

Why? While it was important to me to clearly set the vision for unity, equip my team with clear paths for conflict resolution, and guide them to live into that commitment to unity, I also wanted to identify the mature leaders among us.

There's a scene in the film *Hidden Figures*, about three female African American mathematicians who helped propel NASA's work during the United States and Soviet Union's "space race," that highlights the importance of identifying leadership. When the director of the Space Task Group (STG), Al Harrison, discovers that the head engineer, Paul Stafford, is deliberately discriminating against the math prodigy Katherine Johnson, the only female and African American on the staff, he says, "You know what your job is, Paul? Find the genius among those geniuses. Pull us all up. We get to the peak together, or we don't get there at all."[3]

Oftentimes, we hesitate to identify other leaders because we think our main job as leaders is to make the biggest impact (through control, crowd, or contribution). While we're pursuing that, we can easily see others as distractions, dead weight, or competition, but that couldn't be further from the truth. Our biggest impact is to identify the mature leaders among us. And I might add, considering each unique place where we participate in church and community, it's to identify the mature leaders who look, talk, eat, and live like those in the congregation and the community around us.

I am a Korean American immigrant who has transplanted from the East Coast to Honolulu, Hawaii, where my three kids have grown up. Most Asian Americans in Hawaii are not only mixed-race but also third-, fourth-, fifth-generation Hawaiian Americans from the plantation era of the late 1800s. I am an East-Coaster and academic at heart, and it colors my pacing, interests, and conversations. My job as the senior pastor of this local church based in Hawaii wasn't to do works of service for or on behalf of my congregation; it also wasn't to look for people who were just like me. It was first to equip the congregation for works of service to benefit the *local* community around us, and second to identify the mature *local* leaders among us.

When leaders begin to think that their own leadership (whether it's their decision-making power, spiritual authority, or relational advantage) is threatened, they start seeing their own congregation and community as threats. There is an element of truth in this sentiment though: identifying leaders does feel at times like it pulls you away from doing meaningful ministry work. Sometimes it slows down the pace of ministry. And when someone finally rises to share leadership and the congregation begins to adhere to them, it does feel like they are comparing this new team member to you.

But when those natural tensions and concerns come up in our hearts, we should consider how Jesus led. If his focus was on gaining control, he quite honestly would not have given himself over to be crucified. Crucifixion is the opposite of gaining power: in fact, it was the way he exemplified a new kind of power.[4] In Mark 9, we find the disciples arguing once again about who was the greatest among them. "What were you arguing about on the road?" Jesus asked them. "But they kept quiet because on the way they had argued about who was the greatest. Sitting down, Jesus called the Twelve and said, 'Anyone who wants to be first must be the very last, and the servant of all'" (Mk 9:33-35).

The word *greatest* comes from the Greek word *megas*, which pertains not only to a high physical measurement or quantity of an object but also to a predicated high rank, to be highly esteemed for excellence and importance, essentially, bearing "God's preeminent blessings."[5] The disciples were arguing about who holds the most power, the most control. Jesus turned their vision of greatness to focus on self-giving love, and he modeled it not only by his life and ministry but through the most humiliating loss of power and control.

If Jesus' focus had been on amassing a crowd, he could have succumbed to the will of the people and mobilized them as many of his political and religious counterparts did at that time. He could have settled where he was most popular and built his power base. He could have chosen to form his multitudes in city centers, where most of the religious scribes drew followers. Instead, Jesus stole away from the crowd, moving place to place and often in remote locations. "Yet the news about him spread all the more, so that crowds of people came to hear him and to be healed of their sicknesses. But Jesus often withdrew to lonely places and prayed" (Lk 5:15-16). Jesus showed the disciples repeatedly that leadership had more to do with the personal than the public.

If Jesus' focus was on mounting a list of contributions to make the most impact as a leader, he would have probably started his debut much sooner than thirty years of age (Lk 3:23) and certainly would have extended his ministry of itinerant preacher and healer for much longer than merely three years.[6] In addition, he could have mingled with the most powerful to gain a political or social edge or to impress the right people to get sponsorship. Instead, he mostly spent time traveling with his disciples and being among the disenfranchised, marginalized, and weak in the communities.

> While Jesus was having dinner at Levi's house, many tax collectors and sinners were eating with him and his disciples, for there were many who followed him. When the teachers of the law who were Pharisees saw him eating with the sinners and tax collectors, they asked his disciples: "Why does he eat with tax collectors and sinners?"
>
> On hearing this, Jesus said to them, "It is not the healthy who need a doctor, but the sick. I have not come to call the righteous, but sinners." (Mk 2:15-17)

Jesus wasn't basing his leadership on control, crowd, and contribution; he was basing his leadership on sharing leadership with his disciples. When we look at the life and ministry of Jesus, the biggest impact Jesus made in those three years was on equipping and sending those twelve disciples. Jesus' impact was on identifying leaders. He never saw his disciples as distractions, dead weight, or competition. He was patient with them, lived life with them, equipped and taught them, and loved them to the very end (Jn 13:1).

Even in that first year with my local church, my leadership goal wasn't just to provide a learning environment for my community; it was to identify who also provided a learning environment over a teaching environment for our community. It wasn't to provide a healing environment by myself; it was to identify who also provided a healing environment over a comfortable environment for our community. Who was working alongside me to provide a welcoming environment over an entertaining environment for the sake of our community? Who was already focused on providing a liberating environment over a perfect environment for our community? And who else was working to provide a sending environment over a competitive environment for our community?

In addition, because I expected to find a variety of both immature and mature leaders in the church, I was also looking for people who were growing in and displaying the four Hs: humility, honor, hospitality, and hope. Those who display maturity markers are the types of leaders who are more able to be equipped to become mature APEST leaders. With intentional guidance and time, a humble, honoring, hospitable, and hopeful APEST leader can mature from providing a teaching, comfortable, entertaining, perfect, competitive environment to providing a learning, healing, welcoming, liberating, and sending environment. Identifying leaders also involves equipping leaders in discipleship (leaders are disciples first), marks of maturity (sharing leaders are humble, honoring, hospitable, and hopeful), and cultivating environments (sharing leaders know how to utilize APEST).

KNOW YOUR SKEW

My recommendation for identifying sharing leaders is to first know your skew. Remember, APEST is a tool to help with sharing leadership, not a personality test to box people in. Knowing our congregation's APEST skew helps us begin to identify the potential leaders who stay in the center, stand at the bridge, or hang out at the edge of community. Knowing the skew also helps the leader to be aware of which leadership gifting is abundant and what is lacking.

Using the APEST tool, how is your congregation skewed? How do you know? Does the majority of the congregation value being in the center, standing at the bridge, or hanging out at the edge of community? Does the majority of the congregation value a learning (or immature teaching) environment, a healing (or immature comfortable) environment, a welcoming (or immature entertaining) environment, a liberating (or immature perfect) environment, or a sending (or immature competitive) environment? Using these same APEST tools can help you determine how your leadership team (both staff and volunteer) is skewed.

SHOW YOUR SKEW

Next, show your skew. Let the congregation become aware of its own preferences, where we are rich and where we have a gap in the reflection of Jesus. Key questions are, What kinds of APEST environments do our church members enjoy? What kinds of APEST environments does our community experience? Even if they are immature experiences, such as the Evangelist's shallow entertaining environment or the Prophet's judgmental perfect environment, these still reveal the APEST skew to the congregation.

Using the APEST tool, how can you show your congregation their skew? How can you show your leadership team their skew? Who do they value more, the congregation (being in the center) or the community (hanging out in the edge of community) or both? Whose story do they know more, the church's or the community's? Which church practice is seen as more important, learning the Bible more (Teacher), having deeper church relationships (Shepherd), having more visitors at church (Evangelist), connecting to social justice (Prophet), or starting new initiatives (Apostle)?

PROVIDE ACTIVE SPACES

Then, provide spaces where people can not only see APEST at work but also actively experience together being the church for the sake of the community. Active participation requires creating intentional spaces and situations of leadership for people to live out unity and maturity and their works of service to benefit the community. Create environments where people can participate in (and not just observe) communal and missional living and watch how different people help to contribute to it. It's in these actions (much more than accumulating content) where we identify sharing leaders. We also get to identify people's motivations quickly when they are participating. Even Jesus' disciples, with full participation in his ministry, struggled with envy, missed vision, ideal expectations, and desire for power.

Where are there active spaces for the congregation to learn together? To heal together? To welcome together? To experience God's shalom together? To be sent out together? Where are there active spaces to participate in the center of the congregation, standing at the bridge, and hanging out at the edge of community? Who is working to establish learning, healing, welcoming, liberating, and sending environments?

LOOK FOR MATURITY

Next, we look for maturity. There's an old Hawaiian practice called *kilo*, "a cultural practice in which humans observe quietly and focus on the less obvious, more subtle things in the environment."[7] Most of the time, we look for obvious "leadership" characteristics around control, crowd, and contribution, but when we start paying attention to the less obvious gifts of servant leadership, we can practice *kilo*. Who are the most humble, yet confident-in-God ones in the congregation? Who are the first to celebrate and bestow honor on others? Who are the people who extend hospitality even when it comes at a cost to them? And who have the most enduring hope within the community? In addition to looking for those who are exhibiting the four Hs of maturity, we can also employ *kilo* to recognize those who live into their mature APEST gifting.

Who are the Teachers who aren't grasping for a teaching position or teaching opportunity but are championing learning and inviting the community into God's story? Who are the Shepherds who aren't limiting growth or criticizing change but are activating healing amid discomfort and inviting the church to be reconciled to the community around it? Who are the Evangelists who aren't easily anxious, discouraged, or resistant to conflict but are welcoming with perseverance and patience and inviting the church to live incarnationally with the community? Who are the Prophets who aren't demanding moral perfection or criticizing the church and community but are hopeful that God's kingdom is at hand and are inviting the church and community to experience God's shalom. And who are the Apostles who aren't demanding a fast-paced, outcome-based people but are engaging the congregation at a compassionate pace to live out its missional calling to the community.

During our first six months together, I knew my church's APEST skew: we were very Shepherd and Evangelist heavy, which meant that there was an inevitable tension around who was valued: insiders or outsiders? Should we make a comfortable and safe space or a fun and entertaining space? Should we grow slowly or quickly? Do we fear threats or rejection? Will we overprotect or overappease?

Additionally, during our first six months, I showed the skew. We became equipped not only in conflict resolution and committing ourselves to thick community with one another; we also became more aware of our differences. And we recognized that, most of the time, differences are in preferences and not moral or organizational rights and wrongs. We needed to be aware that there are different preferences in working and living together, and we needed to become aware of these differences before doing work and life together.

After our first six months, we launched our first community gathering, called Open Spaces. To be honest, there wasn't anything new or innovative about it: we hosted a potluck dinner once a week for our community. We set up tables, each with six seats; made sure at least one or two congregants were at each table; delivered word-of-mouth invitations to our neighbors, friends, coworkers, and family, mostly non-Christians; included all age groups from infant to ninety; and had conversations that started with a five-minute community-oriented talk from the front.

We started with a weekly simple gathering for three reasons. First, being consistent with a weekly community dinner showed the community that we were a people of faithfulness. More than anything else, building credibility and community in Hawaii requires consistency, not prestige or flash. Consistency also helps to cultivate predictability and familiarity, and both of these things help to increase participation from those you are hosting. Folks can figure out quickly the rules of engagement in a community. That first year of hosting Open Spaces, we held weekly gatherings averaging fifty persons in the room, sharing a meal and sharing a story together. Our candlelight Christmas gathering held one hundred participants—both Christians and non-Christians, Black, White, Asian, Indigenous, Latino—having conversations about the community, singing "Silent Night" in Hawaiian, and sharing a moment of silence to ask for the peace we all desire.

Second, simplicity meant that the missional community model we were invested in launching was reproducible. Simple structures and methods allow for sharing leadership. We'll dive further into structures in the next chapter, but having an uncomplicated practice provided practical experiences for our team. Hosting a weekly community dinner seems like a different kind of leadership load than preaching a weekly sermon. In fact, from year one to year two, we multiplied into three different missional communities with three different discipleship cores, each committed to a different identified space of mission. Seven years later and we have multiplied into twelve missional communities. We went from serving 50 people to engaging with over 650.

Third, a weekly simple gathering introduces a space for active participation. In Open Spaces, we had an expectation that everyone would participate. The simplicity of the tasks—bringing a potluck dinner to share with the community, setting up tables and chairs, inviting guests, and joining in on the conversation—offered a lot of flexibility and variety that allowed for each person to participate. We had a decentralized pulpit; those five-minute conversation-starter talks were shared by a rotation of people. Some were incredibly inspiring, and others fell flat. But a five-minute talk wasn't the engine that kept the community going; it was the twenty to thirty minutes of sharing a meal and sharing a story bookending those five minutes that propelled the community forward.

I knew my church was skewed Shepherd and Evangelist. I showed my church our skew and equipped them in conflict resolution and honoring and relying on differences to experience the fullness of Christ for ourselves and the community around us. I provided active space for close contact and experience in what it's like to actually do work and life together. All the while, I was looking for the mature leaders among us.

Knowing our APEST skew, showing them our skew, and providing active participation spaces for my church allowed me to employ *kilo* to find the mature ones who could share leadership. I observed all four Hs (at differing levels) in Hanzo and Meli, both born and raised in Hawaii. More than the skill sets of leadership (of which they have a generous share), they exhibited unabashedly more than anyone else humility with full confidence in who they were in Christ (despite the personal struggles of apathy and anxiety). They were the first to be giddy with excitement at stories about other people's successes and missional accomplishments without an ounce of envy. They encouraged the entire community to celebrate together and honor one another, all the while naming our temptation to self-disqualify ourselves or compare ourselves with one another. They were the quickest to grow in hospitality for both congregation and community—one was no more important or valued than the other—and they helped to set the culture of the entire congregation toward loving one another and the community around us. Finally, they were the ones who held the deepest amount of unthwarted, long-suffering, enduring hope. Hanzo is the champion of reminding all of us that God's kingdom, no matter what we do or not do, is ever expanding, and Jesus is always inviting us into it. Meli is the spearhead for helping us to stay connected to the full gospel, which is the hope for all the brokenness in the world.

I also observed in Hanzo and Meli the growing maturity of their APEST. Hanzo, Maui-raised, musician, and undoubtedly the coolest most relaxed person in the room, has a strong Teacher gifting, but he was determined not to exercise his gift for his own gain. Instead, he constantly wanted to include others, equip others, and recognize a gift for teaching in others. Because of Hanzo's desire to share power, we have a Teaching Team in our church: it identifies other Teachers in our midst, equips our Missional Community leaders in teaching and communicating, and discerns what kind of learning environment our church needs to succeed in our communal and missional life together.

Meli, Manoa-raised, lawyer, and undoubtedly the smartest person in the room, has a strong Prophet gifting, but she has never exercised her gift to criticize the church. Instead, unsolicited, she prayed and kept sharing with me what she thought God was saying about our church, Hawaii, and God's kingdom here on earth. Because of Meli's desire to share power, we have a Prayer Team that leads all our missional communities in experiencing a prayer culture that's safe, accessible, and redemptive.

Two roles in the church, those who are gifted in teaching and praying, which are often touted as the most "professional" or "devout" of us in the church, are instead two environments that are set to cultivate a learning and liberating experience for both congregation and community. The four Hs and APEST were both clear tools I used to identify maturing leaders in our midst, the mature ones who will pull us all up and share leadership (see fig. 10.2).

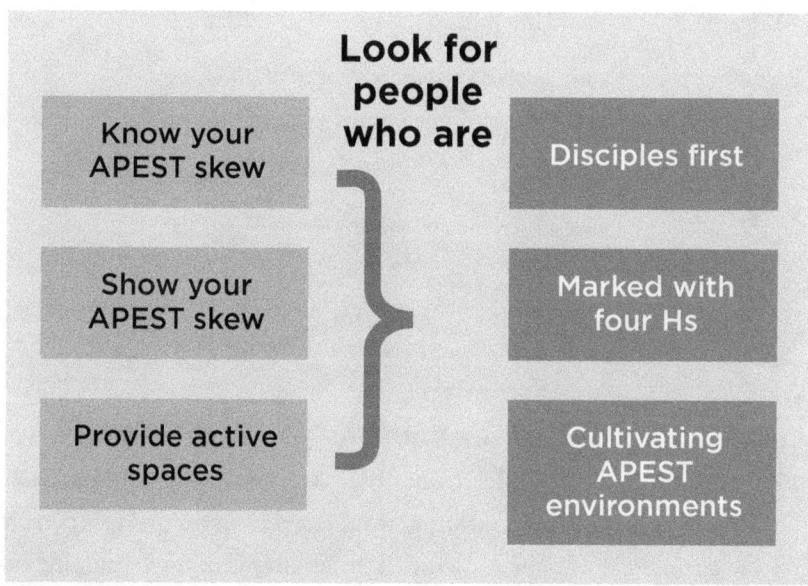

Look for people who are

Know your APEST skew	Disciples first
Show your APEST skew	Marked with four Hs
Provide active spaces	Cultivating APEST environments

Figure 10.2. Identifying maturing leaders

After our first year, when it was time for Amanda to move off island to further her education, she was still as quiet and introverted as ever, but she left me a handwritten note on a brown-paper card. "Thank you for being so inspirational in your leadership; I won't ever forget it. You've welcomed me from the start and helped me see how I truly fit in God's kingdom."

11

HOW TO STRUCTURE SHARING LEADERSHIP

Whatever affects one directly, affects all indirectly.
I can never be what I ought to be until you are what you
ought to be. This is the interrelated structure of reality.

MARTIN LUTHER KING JR.

For just as each of us has one body with many members, and these
members do not all have the same function, so in Christ we, though
many, form one body, and each member belongs to all the others.

ROMANS 12:4-5

"EUN, WE'D LIKE TO OFFER YOU THIS POSITION in shared leadership." I was thrilled at the offer, truly flattered in fact. I thought I had won the jackpot; perhaps this opportunity would never be afforded to a person like me again. A White male-dominant international church-training organization was offering me a place on their shared-leadership executive team. It had been my dream goal to have a seat at the table, helping to represent minority and woman voices and getting a chance to cultivate a growing sense of community within the organization. The first time I led a training session for this organization, many BIPOC women leaders came up to me afterward, teary-eyed, thanking me for offering hope that they too could lead. If an Asian American woman with immigrant roots, who also had a day job and was married with three children, can plant a church, then why couldn't they? I loved the opportunity and connections. Male leaders, mostly White, in the organization also approached me to share in my excitement, expressing anticipation of a fresh change for everyone. They sensed that my new position, making space for others, and the vision to move from a training organization to a collaborative community would be good for them as well. These were my brothers who had been encouraging my own sense of leadership call at a translocal level for many years. I was sincerely met with celebration and congratulations.

Fast forward, and I ended up resigning from this position. Ultimately, I found no increased diversity in gender or race in the organization and no move from training organization to community. Nothing I had set out to do in taking this shared-leadership position happened. It was a painful transition that would require a different space to discuss and preparation for my heart to process the grief. The essential problem was that despite offering me a position in shared leadership, the organization was not prepared for sharing leadership. It did not have the structures in place to share power.

As I was experiencing this lack of sharing leadership, I also observed a church make the radical decision to go from a solo leadership to sharing leadership after it witnessed, alongside the rest of the world, the brutal murder of George Floyd.[1] Christ City Church lives on H Street in the heart of northeast Washington, DC. The history of the neighborhood dates back to the 1840s and is dotted with both flourishing and decline, including the racially charged riots of 1968. The violence that year demolished the predominantly Black neighborhood known to be the cultural and financial center of Black Washington. In the summer of 2020, the White senior pastor of Christ City Church, Matthew, wrote a letter to his congregation asking what kind of response the church should make to racial violence, violence that was not foreign to their beloved community. While the systemic injustice of racism cannot be dismantled overnight, he chose to step down from his position as a White male leader in response to this moment. Subsequently, an Asian American male leader was chosen.

I cried when I read this announcement; I had never experienced this level of mature sharing leadership before. Even from Hawaii, I felt like my own leadership as an Asian American pastor was recognized. Now Christ City Church showcases a diversity in sharing leadership in all areas of ministries, intentionally including all genders, races, and classes.

LEADERSHIP PIPELINES

There are some common criteria for choosing church leaders, resulting in a narrow pipeline to leadership. Most churches, the majority having been started by White male or White-assimilated evangelical leaders, want a leader who is charismatic. They look for a person with an ideal vision, which often is love God, love others, and love yourself. The person must be an excellent communicator, which often means entertaining, knowledgeable, or caring. The church wants a person who can meet the needs of a group of people, a group that is still often individualistic, capitalistic, and homogeneous.

Soong-Chan Rah comments about the leader's pressure to meet the individualistic needs of each congregant,

> The American church, in taking its cues from Western, white culture, has placed at the center of its theology and ecclesiology the primacy of the individual. The cultural captivity of the church has meant that the church is more likely to reflect the individualism of Western philosophy than the value of community found in Scripture. The individualistic philosophy that has shaped Western society, and consequently shaped the American church, reduces Christian faith to a personal, private, and individual faith.[2]

The capitalistic methodology of church planting is strongly oriented around funds. "Most of the guys we identify as high-caliber leaders," said Chad Childress, "raise funds because their vision is so big and they have the leadership capacity to pull it off."[3] Churches often grow with a charismatic pastor who attempts each week to meet the individualistic needs of the spectating congregation. Consequently, churches rise or fall depending on the leader. Because of emphasis on individualism and capitalism, churches expect pastors to be CEOs and the church the product to consume.

In addition, whether we like to admit it or not, race has a crucial part to play in churches. While a 2020 study showed that 16 percent of congregations in the United States identified as multiracial, multiracial most often means White and Black congregants.[4] As Gerardo Martí writes, "The project of creating a multiracial church has become more suspect among some conservative White churches."[5] Korie Edwards says, "These spaces can actually create a good deal of pain for people of color. In many ways, they are expected to assimilate to the dominant White culture. They end up having to hide or let go of their own cultural preferences and minimizing their ethnic and racial identity."[6] Ryan Brooks, a Black pastor of a seven-year-old multicultural church in North Carolina, states, "If you want something to grow very big and very fast, make it extremely comfortable."[7]

When theology and ecclesiology are driven by the culture, then church leadership will mimic the culture. And our culture seeks leaders who will meet our desires for individualism, capitalism, and uniformity. These are the people who fill the traditional pipeline to church leadership. Who are most often invited into leadership? Good charismatic communicators who can wield control, crowd, and contribution to grow the attendance in Sunday services.

When I was leading in a shared-leadership context in a previous church, a similar feeling came to mind: I was the first female pastor to be invited into an executive shared-leadership team for an exciting church-plant opportunity. It was poised for growth. We had every successful church-plant launch model you can think of: resources, talent (both communication and musical), and an army of volunteers. We grew the church from 20 volunteers to 450 weekly Sunday morning attendees in five years. Growth of service attendance was one thing, but I also noticed something else. The pipeline adopted for identifying leadership was skewed. It was definitely an old boys' club. Our church took on the same "mentoring" methodology as older business practices. Sheryl Sandberg explains that in the business world, mentoring and sponsoring relationships often form between individuals who have common interests or when the junior members remind the more senior members of themselves. This means that men will often gravitate toward sponsoring younger men, with whom they connect more naturally. Since there are so many more men at the top of every industry, the proverbial old-boy network continues to flourish.[8]

Sylvia Hewlett and her team reported that 64 percent of senior-level males were hesitant to have mentorship/sponsorship interactions with junior-level females because of what others might think.[9] Leadership development, it seems, denies gender-based opportunity in order to prevent potential sexual harassment or unprofessional sexual conduct. But this comes at the detriment of not only female leaders but also BIPOC leaders, who may also present a threat to White senior-level males who choose to preemptively prevent DEI snafus.

Sandberg continues,

This evasiveness must end. [In the business world], personal connections lead to assignments and promotions, so it needs to be okay for men and women to spend informal time together the same way men can. A senior man and junior man at a bar is seen as mentoring. A senior man and a junior woman at a bar . . . looks like dating. . . . We cannot assume that interactions between men and women have a sexual component. And everyone involved has to make sure to behave professionally so women—and men—feel safe in all settings.[10]

My church at the time practiced similarly in raising up new leaders—male leaders mentored and developed younger male leaders. Pipelines used to foster leadership did not attempt to define gift or maturity criterion but depended primarily on gender. In five years' time, as we added to our Teaching Team, which is *the* coveted leadership platform, we went from two men and one woman (me) to six men and one woman (still me). Bonding for the Teaching Team was increased by frequent late night "hangouts" and spearfishing outings. In other churches and Christian institutions, I have also witnessed cigar smoking, poker playing, and whiskey tasting as ways to increase bonding.

When I began to challenge why this was our leadership pipeline for mentoring, I also noticed that my two male counterparts had experienced the sort of development I had seen elsewhere. An older male pastor took on a group of younger male up-and-coming leaders, including my two colleagues, and mentored them for years. Each was hand picked by this older leader, their only criteria being that they were "chosen." No one questioned why only men were invited in a denomination that allows for the ordination of women and women in leadership. Most of these men have become senior pastors of churches and continue to perpetuate solo-male-dominant leadership and mentorship in the church today.

When we examine the leadership pipelines adopted in non-White churches, we need to consider the origins of most Black, Asian American, Latino, and ethnic-based churches, including my own local multicultural church in Hawaii. Because of historical disenfranchisement, primarily urban settings, and a concentration on the needs of their geographical areas, these churches face a different kind of grasp for power. And grasping for power often determines how power is shared (or not shared). Through my consulting work with Black, Brown, and immigrant churches, I've learned that leaders value the power they gain within the church because it is so hard to attain outside the church. Once they acquire the power of leadership in the church, they do not want to let go of it. Cultural and geographic communities that have been disempowered based on race, gender, sexuality, and class, often with prevalent financial burdens, grasp and hold onto power also. These are the non-White church versions of meeting individualistic needs for cultural self-preservation and perpetuation, using capitalism to gain societal prominence, and homogeneity symbolizing safety and cultural familiarity.

The first-generation Korean American church I grew up in went through a painful split because of power issues. The Presbyterian denomination we raised our children in experienced a painful split because of power issues. My current denomination may experience a painful split because of power issues. I believe that the pain associated with power is preventable or at least approachable if each of these churches and organizations were poised and structured for sharing power.

LEADERSHIP GROWTH STORY

The first thing we need to consider in evaluating candidates for leadership, establishing a pipeline, is to have clarity in our goals for growth. More than anything else, what we want to grow determines the leadership we require. Many churches want to grow church attendance; therefore, leadership development concentrates on the top two leadership hires in the church: a preaching pastor and a worship pastor. The youth and children's pastors come next, only to support the purpose of the main product—hosting a worship service experience that grows church attendance.

In our church, I knew we wanted to grow disciples. In order to do this, I focused on formation (being equipped in discipleship), praxis (having practice spaces to live out discipleship), and examples (experiencing real-life models of disciples). These were the criteria for our pipeline. Just as Paul tells the Jesus communities in Corinth to imitate him as he imitates Christ (1 Cor 11:1), our congregations need leaders who are not just great at speaking or singing. We need leaders who are living out their imitation of Jesus so that the entire congregation is invited into discipleship as both formation and praxis—shaping who they are and how they live.

Because of our intent to center discipleship, we developed a pipeline for leaders for that purpose. Instead of simply increasing the attendance at our fifty-member weekly community dinners, we wanted to multiply a discipleship core that was tethered to an identified space of mission. A discipleship core shaped discipleship formation, and an identified space of mission was where discipleship praxis happened (see fig. 11.1). We called a discipleship core tethered to an identified space of mission a "missional community."[11] In order to multiply more missional communities, I looked for people who were aware of potential neighborhoods and networks for development, other places where Jesus was already at work.

I remember that first year praying, "Jesus, if I just had this first discipleship core to equip and we didn't grow for the next five years, I wouldn't mind it at all. In fact, you didn't multiply your leaders until after three years!" But, to my surprise, this wasn't what God had in mind. He had in mind to grow our church, and he had in mind to grow our church through leaders whose discipleship was shaping who they were and how they lived.

Kelci and Melissa are both Evangelist-Prophet wired in the APEST designations. They are completely different personalities and have extremely different backgrounds and upbringings, but the two of them were the first to multiply our church.

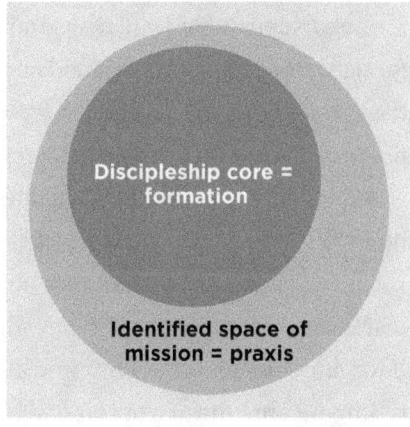

Figure 11.1. Missional community includes discipleship formation and praxis

Kelci is a very fun-loving, petite, blond-haired, blue-eyed transplant from the Midwest. More than anything else, she loves games (and she annoyingly wins most of the time). She happens to be a hospice-care nurse; if you want to see Kelci come alive, just bring her to a nursing home. As she was being formed into more Christlikeness, her discipleship began to shape how she wanted to live like Christ.

In Kelci's bicycle commute to work in her Kaka'ako neighborhood, there are three low-income senior living facilities. In Hawaii we call the elderly *kupuna*, which means "revered ones." Kelci loves her *kupuna* neighbors. After experiencing a charitable work day working at one of these residential facilities, Kelci was the only volunteer who paid attention to how Jesus was inviting her to live. Kelci invited some of the *kupuna* from these low-income facilities to our Open Spaces dinners. At these dinners they enjoyed a home-cooked potluck meal, experienced the gift of a multigenerational community, and had a chance for meaningful conversation in which they could contribute and tell their stories (or "talk-story" as we say in Hawaii).

After that first year, Kelci started her own missional community called Kaka'ako Kupuna. She gathered a group of volunteers who shared her concern for these low-income *kupuna* and began weekly bingo and pizza nights with them in the comfort of their own complex. Kaka'ako Kupuna now serves the needs of five hundred low-income seniors in their neighborhood.

Melissa is a conscientious, Japanese/Mexican/German local who grew up with a single mom on the east side of Oahu. More than anything else, she loves plants; she would undoubtedly confess that she probably loves plants more than people. She's an administrator, married with two young boys, and lives in a condominium on Kahuhipa Street in Kaneohe, a mid- to low-income former Japanese agricultural neighborhood. As she was being formed into more Christlikeness, her discipleship began to shape how she wanted to live like Christ.

If you walked down Kahuhipa Street with Melissa, she could tell you every story about every building, the residents there, what the playground scene is like, what businesses have been there for years and which are new, and the names of the business owners and their family members. There's a scene in the movie *Erin Brockovich* where a new legal firm is trying to take over the case against Pacific Gas and Electric, and the film's namesake, a paralegal, is being questioned by the big-wig lawyers about how much she actually understood the multimillion-dollar case. Erin proves to them how much *more* in fact she knew about the case by reciting many of the six hundred Hinkley, California, plaintiffs' names, phone numbers, children's names, addresses, vocations, and medical diagnoses from memory.[12]

Melissa is the Erin Brockovich of Kahuhipa Street. After inviting some neighbors to our Open Spaces dinners, she realized after that first year that she could do the same thing in her own neighborhood: host a potluck meal and have meaningful conversations as neighbors. But Melissa was also paying attention to how Jesus was inviting her to live. Her discipleship wasn't just about having a community dinner with her neighbors; it was about mobilizing the neighborhood to come together for the sake of the neighborhood. Our Kahuhipa has become a community organization that addresses the needs of their neighborhood's low-income and houseless neighbors.

That first year both Kelci and Melissa started asking questions like, Who are my neighbors? What is God already doing in my neighborhood? How can I join him in his work? We discussed some broad structure for multiplication. For one of our missional communities to start, the leader will have progressed along a discipleship pathway (they're disciples first), identified a space of mission, tried out an intentional rhythm of gathering for at least six months, and worked together or have a plan to work together with a new discipleship core.

After achieving discipleship, Kelci identified a low-income senior living facility and Melissa identified her own condominium as spaces for mission. For six months, Kakaʻako Kupuna hosted regular bingo nights and Our Kahuhipa hosted semimonthly community dinners. They each worked with a discipleship core to implement their plans, completing the steps of formation. Missional community leaders are formed by Christ, live like Christ, and are examples of Christlikeness to others.

It was interesting to see that where community and mission were stressed in developing discipleship, Evangelist-Prophets were first to multiply. They live as a bridge between the congregation and the community and are able to call the community to live toward renewal. Both the sense of belonging for "outsiders" and the sense of purpose for the community were met first in Kelci's and Melissa's leadership. With these successes we knew that we wanted to develop a pipeline for multiplying disciples who were living out mission together. After seven years, our communities have multiplied from one to twelve different missional communities with shared leadership, where discipleship is tethered to renewal.

It's worth noting that while both relationships and tasks are important for community and mission, the ability to make friends and the ability to accomplish things were not the hallmarks of the leaders identified in our pipeline. Neither the desire for popularity nor productivity was in play here. Nor were the leaders chosen based on a skill set (e.g., preaching or leading worship) or capability (efficiency or creativity). The desire for power was also nonexistent in these potential leaders. Community multiplied through leaders whose discipleship (their formation and identity—who they are) was tethered to renewal (their praxis and purpose—how they live). Kelci and Melissa became missional community leaders because Jesus was growing in them a desire to care for their neighbors and care for the renewal of their neighborhoods. Our leadership structure elevated leaders who were incarnational disciples; as the community imitated our leaders, they were imitating Christ. Kelci imitates Christ for the sake of Kaka'ako just as Melissa imitates Christ for the sake of Kahuhipa Street.

STRONG SUPPORT

The metaphor of building a plane while flying it was an accurate image for our pioneering church. As we established a structure for missional community leaders, those whom we wanted the community to imitate, I knew that we also had to structure support for the growing needs of the leaders. Because we multiplied to three missional communities in just one year, leadership began to delineate even further.

Because missional community leaders are not necessarily the best speakers or teachers, we needed another leadership team that helped to clarify our discipleship content, equip the missional community leaders to disciple others through this content, and help identify more Teachers in each of the missional communities to help support the leaders. We developed our Teaching Team (group of three) as a strong support for the missional communities to ask on behalf of our whole church the question, What does God want us to learn about him, about us, and about our community?

Because missional community leaders are not necessarily the most prophetically inclined, we needed another leadership team to help establish a culture of prayer that deeply rooted the missional communities, not just into the community and one another but firmly to God. They equip the missional communities to know and understand God's voice for themselves and others in a way that is safe, accessible, and redemptive. They also pray regularly, not just for each of the leaders and their communities but for the kingdom of God to come to Hawaii. Our Prayer Team (group of three) is a strong support for the missional communities to ask on behalf of our whole church the question, What is God saying to us about himself and his kingdom, about us, and about our community?

Because missional community leaders do not necessarily tend to think of the big picture, we needed another leadership team that helped to keep an eye from higher ground to free up the missional community leaders to do what they're best at, living low to the ground. Our Vision Team (group of five) is a strong support for the missional communities to ask on behalf of our whole church the question, Where is God taking us, how does he want us to grow toward unity and maturity, and who does he want us to partner with?

Even in sharing leadership, each of the Strong Support Teams has a point leader who has a certain APEST that is prioritized. The Teaching Team's main leader has a mature Teacher gift. The Prayer Team's main leader has a Prophet gift. And the Vision Team's main leader has an Apostle gift. Our Strong Support Teams provide a balance for each of the missional communities, especially since most of the missional communities are led by the more relationship-oriented APEST—the Shepherds and the Evangelists. For organizational support, we also have a Communications Team (three people) and a Finance Team (three people) to work alongside the Teaching, Prayer, and Vision Teams to support the missional communities.

Just as the tip of the iceberg is the first visible sign of the glacier beneath the surface, the most visible leaders in our church are the missional community leaders (not the Teaching, Prayer, or Vision Team leaders), those whom we want the community to imitate as they imitate Christ (see fig. 11.2). Even in our quarterly public gatherings of all the missional communities, the support teams serve primarily to equip the missional community leaders. No one leaves these public liturgical gatherings remembering the lead pastor; they all remember the experience of reflecting, lamenting, and hoping together.

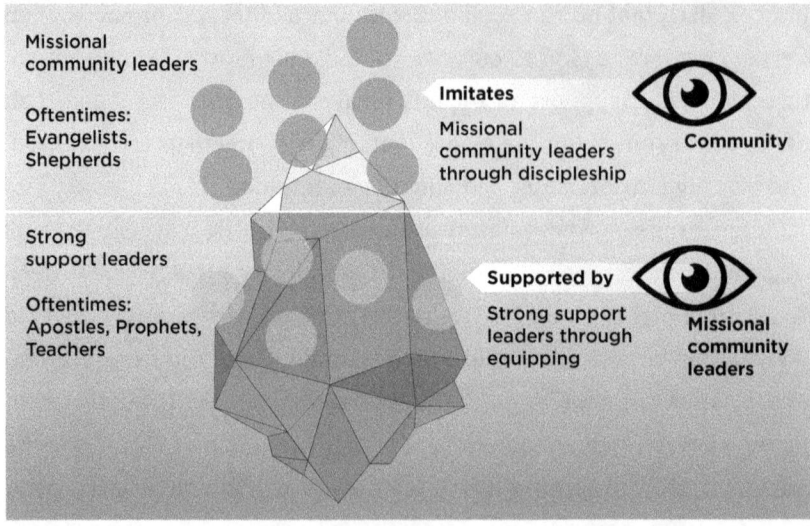

Figure 11.2. Delineation of leadership structure

A key emphasis is the kind of imitation examples we are providing for people. The missional community leaders are the most visible because we want the congregation and community to imitate them in their discipleship, formation, and praxis. The Strong Support is visible to the missional community leaders as we begin to identify more leaders to continue equipping the people of God for works of service, toward unity and maturity, for the flourishing of the community around us.

VOICES AT THE TABLE

What happens within these teams? Even before we started delineating leadership, we made sure to instill a culture of sharing leadership. There was never a single-person leadership; as efficient and faster paced as it could have been, we never forfeited the practice of sharing. We always started with listening prayer—beginning in silence, each of us asking what God would want for our time together. Though following an agenda may seem more productive, we held fast to keeping an open seat at the table for the Holy Spirit. We also practiced making space for each of the APEST by prioritizing which voices at the table went first. For instance, if the topic is personnel or personal relationships, the Shepherds and Evangelists speak first. In discussing partnerships, Apostles and Prophets speak first. Regarding content, Teachers and Prophets. For narrative and communication, Evangelists, Teachers, and Apostles. For congregation discernment, Shepherds and Prophets. On community discernment, Evangelists and Prophets.

Table 11.1. APEST voices at the table

Topic	Make space for this APEST leader first
Personal	Shepherd, Evangelist
Partnership	Apostle, Prophet
Content	Teacher, Prophet
Communication	Evangelist, Teacher, Apostle
Congregation discernment	Shepherd, Teacher, Prophet
Community discernment	Evangelist, Prophet, Apostle

When there are disagreements, we practice asking one another questions such as, What might you be guarding? What value are we missing? Whose voice are we missing at this table? Most of the time, Apostles are guarding movement, Prophets wondering about motivation, Evangelists considering the moment, Shepherds valuing mending, and Teachers what's shaping our minds (see table 11.2).

Table 11.2. APEST guarding

APEST	What might you be guarding?
Apostle	Movement
Prophet	Motivation
Evangelist	Moment
Shepherd	Mending
Teacher	Mind

In addition to APEST voices, congregational and community voices need to be represented in the decision-making process. We also consider that different people process differently—we make sure to carve out time for processing before people chime into a discussion (to the chagrin of extroverted leaders). When big decisions need to be made that will affect the entire church, we make sure to have a six-month lead time and a six-month lag time. This allows time to prepare and process with the leaders and time to evaluate possible losses and gains. These structures within meetings have cultivated sharing leadership at all levels of leadership teams (see fig. 11.3).

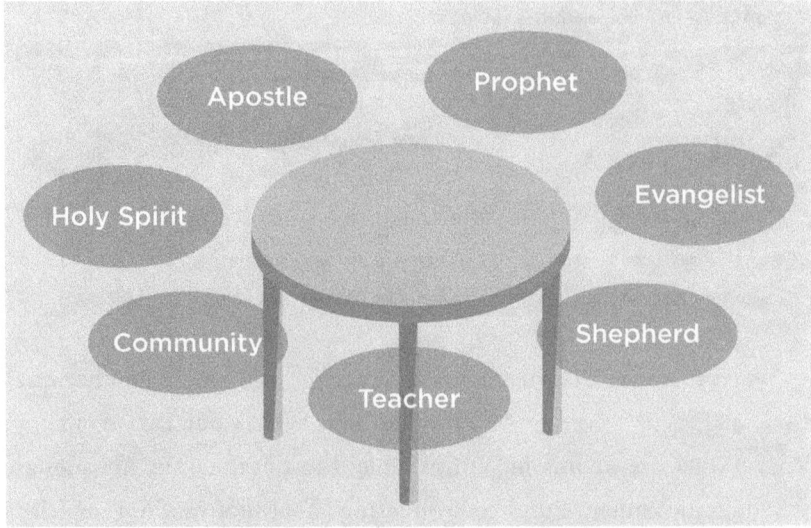

Figure 11.3. Voices at the table

DELINEATION OF LEADERSHIP

Delineation of leadership is the single most painful and difficult process a congregation goes through—particularly a congregation that holds space for participants and not spectators. Leadership delineation is a desirable trait in spectator churches because the congregation seeks to feel safe or feel special through the delineated leader. On the other hand, when a church is full of participants, delineation of leadership at best feels unfair and at worst like prejudice. It is a tender path to navigate but one that is necessary in order to share leadership.

Even when our church was multiplying from one missional community to three, there actually wasn't an air of excitement—there was foreboding. Why do we need to change? Everything's going fine, great in fact. We're going too quickly! Why Kelci? Why Melissa? It's going to be too much of a disruption. People need to get closer not farther apart! We're not ready.

It's easy for leaders to label an uncertain or unprepared people as unwilling to change, stubborn, unimaginative, stuck. The truth is that people will often resist change for two simple reasons: loss and being lost. They will either fear losing something of great value to them that is worth protecting, or they will fear that they themselves are being thrown to the wayside because they may not be able to fully participate and adapt to change.

My congregation wasn't fearful of change; they were processing loss. Our first year, being deeply discipled together in our discipleship core and working side by side in Open Spaces was a profound experience. There was an unplumbed level of work that God was doing in all of us, through us, and around us. Our final Open Spaces community dinner hosted a hundred people of all ages, both Christians and non-Christians, at table together continuing to have meaningful conversations about the community. Children with disabilities were welcomed. Seniors who had difficulty ambulating were surrounded by community. Families, business owners, coworkers, neighbors, baristas, local folks, and military personnel participated. We celebrated one whole year together with games, a photo booth, music, and talk-story. The evening was filled with both quiet reflection and laughter. We laughed so much that night. Why would we want to lose this?

This is when maturity and vision are so vital to the life of a church. Mature leaders help the community look at the vision. Those who exhibit humility, honor, hospitality, and hope are the ones who will help the congregation navigate change and growth. Those who constantly, compassionately, and consistently share the vision of a growing and flourishing kingdom of God that isn't limited to us encourage growth. Those who help the congregation sort out the falsities of an idealized community, personal needs, proximity to power, and anticipated routes to leadership guide a community through change to something new and greater. They're the ones, like Kelci and Melissa, who are multiplying leadership, not for their own gain but for the sake of more communities being able to experience the belonging and purpose of God's kingdom.

12

HOW TO SUSTAIN SHARING LEADERSHIP

Thus the activity of preservation should be distinguished from the nostalgia accompanying fantasies of a lost home from which the subject is separated and to which he seeks to return. Preservation entails remembrance, which is quite different from nostalgia.

IRIS MARION YOUNG

*His miracles are staggering,
his wonders are surprising.
His kingdom lasts and lasts,
his sovereign rule goes on forever.*

DANIEL 4:3 THE MESSAGE

WHEN STARTING ANYTHING NEW, most organizations, both for-profits and nonprofits, adhere to three key points:

- The deliverable: What is the service, content, or product? What is the thing that solves the problem or meets the identified need?
- Feasibility: Can it be done? What do we need in materials, tools, training, environment, resources, etc. to make it a reality?
- Sustainability: How long will it last? What do we need to keep it going?

While the church should be cautious in mimicking business models, there are invaluable parallels to highlight. These questions regarding deliverables, feasibility, and sustainability are questions that church leaders should also be asking.

When we contrast a hierarchical leadership model with a framework for sharing leadership in the church, there is a gap in vision. Hierarchical leadership, with the goals of church growth and meeting an ideal community, deliverables are sermons and social availability. Feasibility is maintained through Sunday worship services and meeting the ABCs of church.[1] Sustainability, concern for how long this enterprise will last and how we keep it going, is addressed by maintaining status quo and resisting change.

In contrast, sharing leadership has the goal of equipping the people of God for works of service. The deliverable is discipleship, that is, equipping the church to imitate Jesus. Feasibility is bolstered by deep commitment to communal life and the unity of a diverse community. Sustainability is achieved by answering these questions: Do we need to exist? For whom do we need to exist? In essence, sharing leadership that equips the church for the works of service through Christlike self-giving love resides with the community to benefit the city, community, and neighborhood. The sustainability of the church lies in how much the church participates in the life of the community.

Kyuboem Lee, professor of missiology at Missio Seminary, reflects on the need for change:

> The unstated but nonetheless real goal of many churches is to be relevant, visible, influential, wealthy, powerful, "for the sake of Jesus," of course, but the means have a sneaky tendency to become the ends rather quickly. Such systems are not interested in reinvention of the church for the sake of mission in our time; they are interested in protecting the systemic status quo and those in positions of power. They often pine for the days when the church used to be powerful and respected; they often misremember those times as times when the gospel was believed and lived. The reality, as Black Christians remind us, was quite different.

These theologies and systems reflexively take us backward and resist new opportunities for mission and transformation. Crises should reveal that these systems do not work, at least not to serve kingdom purposes, and we need reform. Our nostalgia and commitment to these systems keep us from seeing this and hold us back.[2]

Jonathan "Pastah J" Brooks writes about his ministry commitment to the South Side of Chicago:

Jon Fuller, while director of the Overseas Missionary Fellowship, said, "There are no God-forsaken places, just church-forsaken places." While he was speaking of the church being absent in some of the remotest places in the world, I echo that sentiment for the neglected neighborhoods in cities right here in America. Don't get me wrong: there is no shortage of established church buildings or new congregations being planted in these communities. However, there is a shortage of community ownership and genuine church partnership resulting in community transformation. The church often exists in these communities either as fortresses built to keep the struggles of the community on the outside or as patronizing social-service entities prescribing answers for a community without ever listening.[3]

Sharing leadership in the church is only sustainable as the sharing leadership connects the congregation to the community. If the community in which the church resides is not participating in the flourishing of God, then the people of God are not being equipped for works of service. There is no unity of the church nor communal maturity happening if the cities, communities, and neighborhoods are not benefiting from the sacrificial life of the people of God.

DISCIPLESHIP AND SHARING LEADERSHIP

While I also believe in the priesthood of all believers (1 Pet 2:5-9), we start with leadership because they are the ones doing the work of equipping the priesthood of all believers. The people of God to do the work of God in the world that God loves. For sharing leadership to be sustainable, mature APEST leaders who are full of humility, honor, hospitality, and hope must focus on discipling the congregation. Not just teach them, care for them, invite them, free them, or send them but equip them to be more like Christ and live like Christ.

Sustainability questions I often ask leaders are, Five years from now, what do you imagine your church will be like? What will your people be like and participate in? What will your church look like, sound like, feel like? Five years is short enough to be a foreseeable future but long enough that leaders can prepare for it now. Most leaders are at a loss for words and often reply with a reference to the spiritual health of the congregation and numerical growth of the church. This sustainability question exposes in leaders what they are desiring and what their vision is for the church.

I know when discipleship is at the periphery of a leader's vision for their church when (1) discipleship is not included in voicing their hope for the church in five years and (2) the flourishing of the neighborhood or surrounding community of the church is not included (see fig. 12.1). Leaders with discipleship at the periphery of their vision believe that the church service (sermon and worship experience) will effectively address intimacy with God, personal wholeness, deep connection with others, and participation in renewal of the community. And they will assume that this will work because their congregants will be more spiritually healthy (without knowing how to name criteria for this) and church attendance will increase.

On the contrary, when leaders focus on discipleship, their central concern will be to equip the congregation to imitate Jesus together (see fig. 12.2). Discipleship will equip the congregation to experience intimacy with God. Discipleship will equip the congregation to address their personal wholeness. Discipleship will equip the congregation to know how to have deep connection with others. And discipleship will equip the congregation to participate in the renewal of the community.

It takes sharing leadership to center discipleship in equipping the congregation. It takes a combination of mature APEST leaders to *equip* the church and not do the work for the congregation. Immature church leaders get stuck providing the conduit through which the church experiences intimacy with God because they

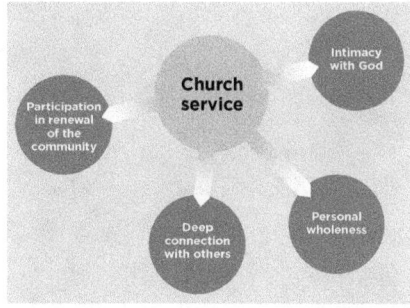

Figure 12.1. Discipleship at periphery

succumb to a church's expectation (see fig. 12.3). A church may become dependent on the immature leader in seeking their personal wholeness. The immature leader may give in to the church members' longing to make a deep connection with the leader. The church may demand that the leader provide primary leadership for any engagement with those outside the church walls. When we don't clarify that the leader's call is not to do for

the church but to equip the church, then often the leader becomes the center of the structure and the church becomes dependent on the leader. Dependency screams out lack of maturity. Dependency also screams out lack of community, which means that the church is not living into unity.

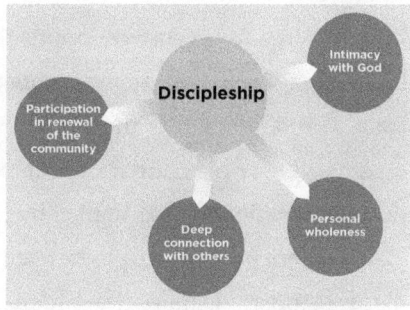

Figure 12.2. Discipleship as central

In Ephesians 4, Paul talks about where the body of Christ is headed. The APEST equips the body of Christ for works of service *until.* Until what? Until when? "Until we all reach unity in the faith and in the knowledge of the Son of God and become mature, attaining to the whole measure of the fullness of Christ" (Eph 4:13). APEST leaders strive to equip the body of Christ until we all communally live in unity and maturity so that we can reflect to the world around us the fullness of Jesus—that he is truly the good news we all

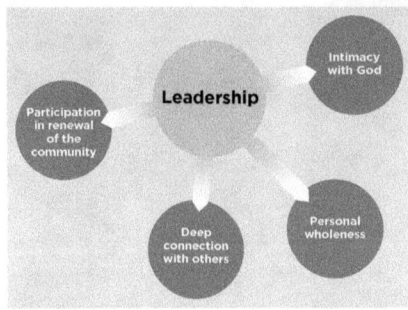

Figure 12.3. Leadership as central creates dependency

have been waiting for. Therefore, APEST leaders work to work ourselves out of a job.

Mature humble, honoring, hospitable, and hopeful APEST leaders have learned to work with the community to turn toward Christ. Mature Teacher leaders don't focus on teaching; instead, they focus on equipping the congregation to be discipled by establishing learning environments, places where people teach and learn from one another. Mature Shepherd leaders don't focus on just caring for the church or making people feel comfortable; instead, they focus on equipping the congregation to be discipled by establishing healing environments, places where people experience healing together. Mature Evangelist leaders don't focus on entertaining or doing all the inviting; instead, they focus on equipping the congregation to be discipled by establishing welcoming environments, places where people grow in invitation and hospitality themselves. Mature Prophet leaders don't focus on making sure the church is righteous; instead, they focus on equipping the congregation to be discipled by establishing liberating environments, places where people grow to be agents of righteousness themselves. And mature Apostle leaders don't focus on growth; instead, they focus on equipping the congregation to be discipled by establishing sending environments, places where people can identify in one another their calling and purpose.

Teachers who do all the teaching will run out of material, become out of fashion, or cause the congregation to depend on one person for learning. Shepherds who do all the caring will run out of steam, run out of patience, or disappoint others because they will never meet the individualistic needs of the congregation. Evangelists who do all of the inviting and entertaining will be discouraged, experience rejection, and lose the crowd. Prophets who do all the justice and prayer work will become angry and disappointed with the congregation and judge them. Apostles who do all the sending and calling work will grow in resentment and boredom and eventually outpace the congregation. All these approaches are not sustainable because they all lead to burnout.

Discipling and equipping the church require sharing leadership. Sharing leadership requires mature leaders who aren't doing all the work for the people of God; instead, mature leaders cultivate environments where the people of God are equipped for works of service that include the community in its flourishing through sending, liberating, welcoming, healing, and learning environments. Sharing leaders do not become overwhelmed because they collaborate across APEST gifting—they are not required to *do* everything.

COMMUNITY AND SHARING LEADERSHIP

A deep commitment to communal life and the unity of a diverse set of people also contributes to sustainability. This is where the four Hs come most into play in sharing leadership. It's with humility, honoring others, exhibiting hospitality, and reorienting to hope over and over again that the congregation experiences a community that engenders flourishing. Christine Pohl tells us,

> Communities in which we grow and flourish, however, last over time and are built by people who are faithful to one another and committed to a shared purpose. Community life certainly has moments of incredible beauty and intense personal connection, but much of it is daily and ordinary. Our lives are knit together not so much by intense feeling as by shared history, tasks, commitments, stories, and sacrifices.[4]

The way we treat and love one another is what contributes to sustainability more than the tasks we do together. Alan Kreider writes about the first-century church, "The Christians' focus was not on 'saving' people or recruiting them; it was on living faithfully—in the belief that when people's lives are rehabituated in the way of Jesus, others will want to join them."[5] Living faithfully together over the long haul through many ordinary moments, navigating tensions, and practicing self-giving love with one another and the community around us sustains relationships. Sharing leadership is required to sustain this kind of intentional living because the work of equipping the church for the works of service toward unity and communal maturity helps to actively link the congregation's deep communal life to the flourishing of the community around it.

In our local church, we equip our congregation to understand that our deep communal living (what we call living in "thick community") leads to redemptive living (or the flourishing of everyone and everything around us through sacrificial love; see fig. 12.4). Each person who participates in our church is actively experiencing personal restoration and reformation: our broken identity and broken purpose are both healed and transformed to new identity and kingdom purpose. It takes sharing leadership to equip each person to live this out. At a congregational level, the whole church then begins to participate in renewal: fresh work and momentum that are the sign, foretaste, and instrument of the kingdom of God.[6] As the congregation experiences renewal, it is made visible to the community it resides in. At a larger community level, the culture and neighborhood around the congregation begin to participate in awakening—the overflow from the renewal work that transforms the culture and society at large (see fig. 12.4). It takes sharing leadership to equip the church to be connected to the community.

In the previous chapter, I shared how Kelci and Melissa led and multiplied our first missional communities, expanding our church from one missional community to three in one year's time. Let me tell you now about how sustainability works when we connect the church to a community that leads to redemptive living.

As Kelci led Kaka'ako Kupuna, each of her discipleship core (DC) members started to experience personal restoration and reformation as they actively participated in being discipled together and being on mission together to serve the *kupuna* in a low-income senior living facility. As they started to host weekly bingo and pizza nights for the seniors, a congregation formed in which deep communal living started to become a sign, foretaste, and instrument of the kingdom of God in that building. Where residents used to keep their doors closed, doors started staying open. Neighbors started to share resources with one another. There were more stops along the common area for moments of conversation. It became less like a senior living facility and more like a college dormitory! Kelci shared this story of one of the residents:

> In fact, one of the grandmothers—she's Buddhist and regularly attends the dinners—asked one time if she could say grace before the meal. All the Christians in the room were a little surprised, but we said, "Of course!" The grandmother then shared that she noticed that we referred to God as "father" when we prayed, and she had never considered God as Father. She wanted to give it a try. As soon as she prayed, "Father . . . ," she started to weep.

Kelci concluded her story by describing the congregation—young volunteers who loved the elderly and the elderly neighbors, both Christians and non-Christians—gathering around the woman and helping her finish her prayer. We knew that the congregation was beginning to experience renewal.

When the pandemic hit and all gatherings were shut down, Kakaʻako Kupuna transformed into a renewal machine. It mobilized over a hundred volunteers to provide one month's worth of groceries for all the residents in that one facility; the seniors were astounded. Because of the renewal work that God was already doing in that building, in a season when the most marginalized people in society ought to have been left out or dismissed, the seniors in this building experienced renewal together. But it didn't stop there: Kakaʻako Kupuna multiplied to two more missional communities during the pandemic. They provided one month's worth of groceries to all five hundred seniors living in three low-income senior living facilities in the Kakaʻako neighborhood. Kelci now leads

REDEMPTIVE LIVING

Community — AWAKENING — Overflow from renewal work that transforms the culture and society at large

Congregation — RENEWAL — Deep communal living that is the sign, foretaste, and instrument of the kingdom of God

Personal — RESTORATION + REFORMATION — Broken identity and broken purpose are both healed and transformed to new identity and kingdom purpose

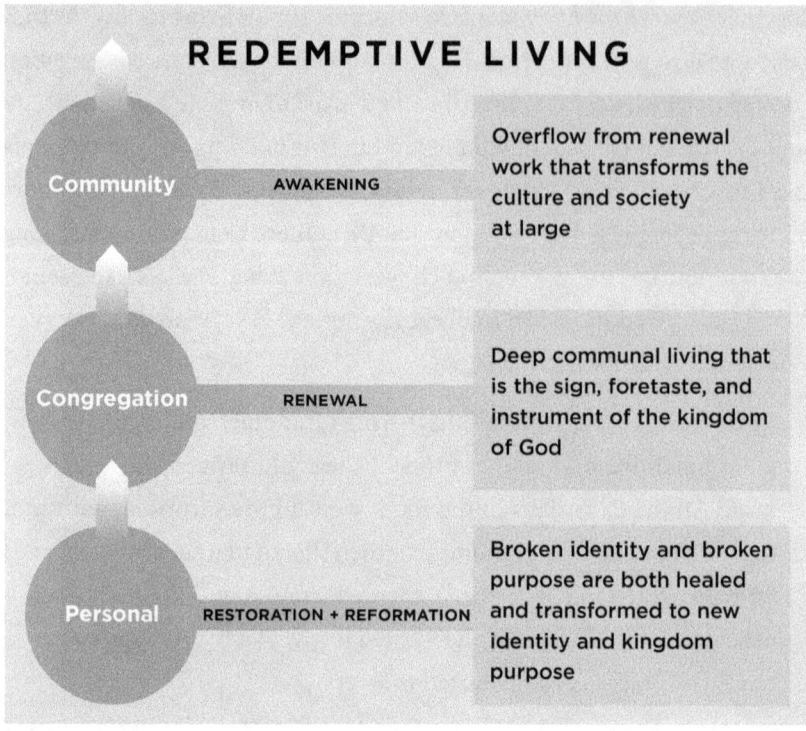

Figure 12.4. Redemptive living

teams of people who lead with the seniors in both communal life and discipleship, the residents of each building experiencing renewal of their own.

But then, something curious happened. The city and county of Honolulu reached out to Kelci to inquire about what she was doing that made these three residential facilities flourish? They wanted to invite her teams to help provide for all nine low-income senior facilities in the area. The work of renewal that was happening inside Kakaʻako Kupuna was being made visible to the outside community. We realized that the culture was experiencing an awakening; the renewal work within the congregation was overflowing into the community and inviting them to be transformed.

Likewise, as Melissa led Our Kahuhipa, each of her disciples was beginning to experience personal restoration and reformation through discipleship. The group of Jesus-following neighbors began to meet regularly to pray for their condominium. They hosted twice-a-month community dinners in the open-air common area to share a meal and share stories together about their neighborhood. Melissa described her experience:

> When Covid hit, we didn't skip a beat! We kept hosting community talk-story times, socially distanced. Each resident, both Christians and non-Christians, pulled up a dining chair or beach chair, propped it by their front door, received a bottle of wine from me, and started our "Wine about Covid" conversations.

They discovered that one of their neighbors, someone they had never seen before, was a Japanese national married to a local Hawaiian man. She was embarrassed and isolated because she did not speak English well. Lo and behold, one of the longtime residents piped up from her beach chair by her front door and began speaking to her in fluent Japanese. They lived just a few doors down from one another. You'll recall that I told you Melissa's condominium sits on Kahuhipa Street, a former Japanese farming neighborhood. These neighbors began to have regular English lessons and Japanese conversations together. Then, the whole floor of the condominium started receiving beautifully packaged home-made Japanese baked goods by their front doors. Neighbors swapped essentials, shared their produce and groceries, and no one was in need. We knew that renewal was happening, a sign, foretaste, and instrument of the kingdom of God on Kahuhipa Street.

It didn't stop there. As the congregation began to have conversations about their neighborhood, they started asking God together, Who are our neighbors? Where are you already at work? How would you like us to join you? Consequently, they paid attention when their school district announced that on average one thousand families with children in grades kindergarten through eighth grade were below the poverty line and started school each year with very limited school supplies.

They went to work and mobilized over a hundred volunteers from their neighborhood to provide brand-new school supplies inside brand-new backpacks to meet 50 percent of the demographic need. Within three years, Melissa led Our Kahuhipa to meet 100 percent of their school district's need to provide for one thousand families. Can you imagine what it's like for a first grader with very few means, whose family often has to decide whether to put food on the table or buy a box of crayons, to receive a fully stocked brand-new school bag? And not just once, but three years in a row?

The work of renewal that was happening inside Our Kahuhipa was made visible to the outside community. Again, the city and county of Honolulu and members of the community were asking how they could mimic what Melissa and her team were doing to meet the educational needs of students in other low-mid-income districts in Oahu. We realized that the culture was experiencing an awakening; the renewal work within the congregation was overflowing into the community and inviting them to be transformed.

All of this happened because Kelci and Melissa were equipped through discipleship and equipped to connect the church to community. They recognized that the flourishing of the church must include the flourishing of the surrounding community. It took (and continues to take) sharing leadership for this kind of missional work to be sustainable.

MISSION AND SHARING LEADERSHIP

When sharing leaders equip the congregation through discipleship that connects the church to the community, it participates in the work of the *missio Dei*. God is a missional and sending God. As the Father sends the Son and together they send the Holy Spirit, so the triune God sends his image bearers to be a sign, foretaste, and instrument of the kingdom of God. Mission answers the sustainability questions: Why does our church exist? Who does our church exist for? Kakaʻako Kupuna exists for the low-income seniors in the Kakaʻako neighborhood. Their vision is for "our *kupuna* [seniors] in Kakaʻako to know that they are seen and loved," and their mission is to create safe and loved communities for the residents in these senior living facilities in Kakaʻako. That mission is fulfilled by helping to address their physical, mental, emotional, and spiritual needs. Our Kahuhipa exists for the neighbors who live on Kahuhipa Street. Our Kahuhipa's vision is that "together as neighbors, we create a community that reflects aloha [deep love] for all," and their mission is to create a neighborhood that brings good change, sincere welcome, and deep care for all neighbors on Kahuhipa Street.

How does sharing leadership connect the church to community? How does sharing leadership practically connect God's people to God's mission? As Dietrich Bonhoeffer writes, "Christianity without discipleship is Christianity without Christ."[7] I like to extend this by adding that discipleship without mission is discipleship without Christ. If leaders are equipping the church to imitate Jesus, then the church will, by default, imitate the way Jesus lived missionally.

The typical strategy for interacting with the community is this: the church invites the community to come to church. The measure of success is whether the church grows. The assumption is that if the church doesn't grow, then we are not interacting with the community correctly. The only way that this model is sustainable is to have the leader focus on designing a church environment that makes the community want to attend. Leaders become effective event planners at best and shallow appeasers at worst. The church will not consider challenging the community because it does not want to offend it and discourage attendance.

Another strategy, though far less often enacted than the model of inviting the community to the church, is the model of having the church go to the community. The measure of success is often measured in how many times the congregation departs the church and runs a community event. The frequency is sparse and is widely used during the holidays when charitable activities are high. Alternatively, churches identify a community to support, often one at a distance from them and recommended by their mission boards (or equivalent), meeting the requirement of sending the church by supporting an overseas missionary. Once again, leaders become effective event planners or good missionary identifiers at best. At worst, they develop unengaged check-the-box-at-Christmastime members.

When I work with church plants and established churches, leaders commonly ask, How do we get our church more engaged with the community? How can our church be sustainable if we concentrate most of our attention on community engagement?

These are earnest questions that tell me these leaders are thinking about ways to connect their churches to the community. They are asking the vital question, Does the existence of our church matter to the community around us? This is where my response may seem surprising: the work of connecting the church to the community is not to send the church into the community. The leader's work is to connect the church to the community and the community to the church (see fig. 12.5).

It's a two-way street. Bridging happens when both the congregation and the community have access to one another. My husband and I once took a

Figure 12.5. Church and community are connected

tandem bicycle ride from Manhattan to Brooklyn over the Brooklyn Bridge. The bridge was covered with bumper-to-bumper traffic—in the car lanes, on the pedestrian lane, and in the cyclist lanes. Steve, an accomplished cyclist who's a triathlete, was sweating bullets after that bike ride because of the insane amount of people traversing the bridge (not to mention his wife's terrified yelps from the back at every sudden stop and pivot). That busy Brooklyn Bridge tells me that both neighborhoods are tightly connected. It's the same with the church and community. The more both the church and community traverse that bridge, the more tightly connected the church is to the community and vice versa.

The concept of a bridge is often misunderstood by the congregation (and perhaps the leader) to mean that the leader must build the bridge between the church and the community. It's perceived to be the leader's job to invite the community to church or to invite the church to the community. If the community isn't coming to church, it's the leader's fault. And if the church is not going out into the community, guess what? It's the leader's fault.

However, in sharing leadership the leaders' clear focus is on equipping and discipling the congregation to do the works of service for the benefit of the community. The bridge is built not by the leader but by the disciples (see fig. 12.6). Sharing leaders expect that as the congregation becomes equipped to be imitators of Jesus, they will, by default, be the ones who connect the church to the community and community to church. There will be an ebb and flow of hosting and being guests with our neighbors. And the metric of success isn't on the numerical growth of the church: it will be on the flourishing of both the church and the community (see fig. 12.7).

Civil rights activist John Perkins states, "We partner alongside God and our neighbors in the places they are already working to bring shalom to our communities—aspiring to make them places where *nothing is missing and nothing is broken*."[8] Flourishing of the church includes the flourishing of the community.

Then, where are the leaders? How does sharing leadership operate in this structure? When we revisit where each of the APEST leaders is positioned in the dynamic life of the church and community, we see that Shepherds and Teachers stand in the

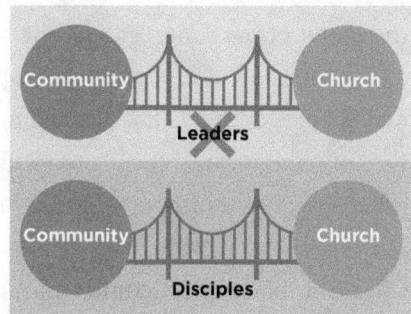

Figure 12.6. Disciples, not leaders, are the connecting bridge

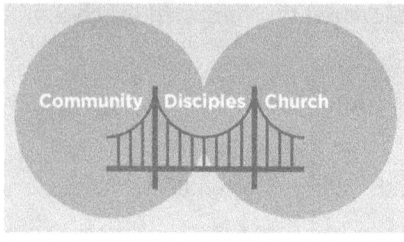

Figure 12.7. Flourishing of the church includes flourishing of the community through discipleship

center of the congregation, the Evangelists stand in the middle of congregation and community, and Prophets and Apostles hang out at the edge of community. Where each of the APEST leaders stands allows all to fully live into their equipping gifts— to equip the congregation for works of service toward unity and communal maturity that benefit the surrounding community.

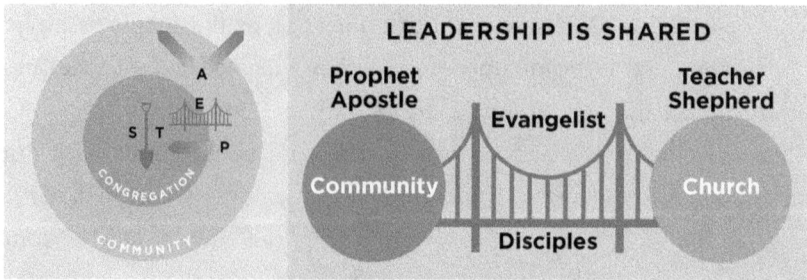

Figure 12.8. Sharing leadership equips disciples to connect the church to the community

When we set figure 7.2 from the earlier chapter next our bridge diagram (see fig. 12.8), we can see the position of each APEST leader. Leadership is shared because we can't be everywhere at once. And each place, the center of the congregation, the bridge, and the community, requires a different kind of discipleship equipping for the church. When Teacher and Shepherd leaders are deemed more important than the others, then the flourishing of just the church will be its goal. When Evangelist leaders are deemed more important than others, then neither the community nor the church will know how to flourish despite being connected; there will be no place to welcome either the congregation or the community. When Prophet and Apostle leaders are seen as more important, then the community will be highlighted but won't be connected to the church, nor the church invited into what God is already doing in the world around them. Mature APEST leadership requires sharing leaders who exhibit profound humility, honor, hospitality, and hope and are willing to live further into *kenōsis*, self-giving love, in order to equip the church for a deep communal life for the flourishing of their neighborhoods and communities.

SHARING LEADERSHIP IN REAL LIFE

Sharing leadership allows the church to be its full self and powerfully include its neighborhood in God's good work, as Jonathan Tran describes:

> The ecosystem includes neighbors and neighborhood businesses, schools, churches, public and private institutions, and all their hopes and dreams and the pressures racial capitalism exerts on them. And it includes God: "What we recognize is that God has been here at work for a long, long time, so we really see ourselves as participating in the work of God."[9]

In 1978, a small group of neighbors (mostly high school students who started a sports-based youth group) on the West Side of Chicago formed Lawndale Community Church. This fifteen-member congregation started asking their neighbors questions about what their community needed. At the top of the list were access to affordable quality healthcare and a full-sized basketball court for the community. Remember, it was a group of teenage athletes, many with single mothers who were caring for multiple younger siblings. The crime rate in this part of the city is 198 percent higher than the Chicago average, the median household income is $26,214, and 92 percent of its adult population hold a high school diploma or less.[10] When the church acquired an old dilapidated building, they began to work with their neighbors to transform it into a worship space, a small health-care clinic, and a full-sized basketball court. Ada Mary of the Chicago Community Trust, being deeply moved by the church's actions, said, "Never in all our years had we seen a grassroots community effort make something like this happen. When we learned that thirty high school kids had donated their spring breaks, we wanted to do all we could to help."[11] The trust donated $150,000 for the efforts of the community center. Today, thirty years later, the Lawndale Community Health Center boasts six state-of-the-art clinics with over a hundred medical providers who also moved into the community, working in one of the most disenfranchised neighborhoods in Chicago. The community also established an affordable health food café, a legal center, an aquaponics farm-to-table garden, and a development corporation to address affordable housing, all focusing on the needs of the North Lawndale neighborhood.

I once took a group of my local leaders from Hawaii on a walking tour of Lawndale Christian Health Center (LCHC). Dr. Wayne Detmer, chief clinical officer of operations at LCHC, was our gracious guide. He's tall, White, an exuberant talker who runs by the seat of his pants and tears up talking about Jesus. As we were touring their incredible facilities and hearing these far more incredible stories of how the church connected to the community, I couldn't help but notice how often Dr. Detmer was stopped in the middle of the street by neighbors. Teens riding bicycles over potholes. Cars moving through intersections. Store owners. Patients. Black, Latino, White, and Asian residents. Each calling out with a big wave of the hand, exchanging intimate niceties about family and health. Lawndale Church wasn't a one-way street to the Lawndale community. A bridge was built so tightly that you couldn't tell the difference between the church and the community.

It takes sharing leadership to hold such a big vision and canvas for the church and community. It takes sharing leadership to make that kind of commitment to one another and to the community for the long haul. It takes sharing leadership to equip the people of God to be a sustainable presence of flourishing for and with their neighbors.

May every church be equipped in discipleship to work alongside their community for the flourishing of their whole neighborhoods, towns, and cities. May every church be equipped to be the full communal reflection of Jesus, sharing his beauty, justice, goodness, wisdom, and righteousness by having concern for one another. May every church be equipped through sending, liberating, welcoming, healing, and learning environments. Therefore, may every church be equipped by the gift of mature sharing leaders. Amen.

EPILOGUE

RICHARD ROHR WRITES, "Those who are not true leaders will just affirm people at their own immature level."[1] If Rohr is correct, then the contemporary church appears to be filled with false leaders pastoring immature but appeased congregations. True leadership is difficult precisely because its intent is not to affirm immaturity but to equip people into maturity. What's more, for the church, maturity is communal; therefore, maturity is linked tightly to unity. And maturity and unity take time, relational ties, faithful presence, difficult conversations, repetitive celebrating, willingness to commit amid difficult personal interactions, and hard work on efforts that sometimes go awry. While maturity and unity are practiced in mission together, for the church, maturity and unity are often attained through commitment to being in relationship with one another.

The communal piece is tricky, because it walks a fine line: the Christian community should never be an idealized desire nor a gathering that furthers isolation. Maturity and unity in the life of the communal people of God require becoming interdependent imitators of Jesus. Deeply dependent on Christ, the church lives into *kenōsis*, self-emptying and self-giving love toward one another. Independent of *harpagmos*, or grasping power for our own gain, the church lives for the flourishing of the community it resides in. These are the two sides of the coin of communal interdependence.

Ultimately, sharing leadership is about equipping the church to experience maturity and unity through living dynamically in this tension. Living communally into this tension requires practice as an outside community constantly watches how we treat one another because they will wonder if we would treat them the same.

In August 2023, just two weeks after the devastating fires ravaged West Maui, I wrote this letter to my church, Ma Ke Alo o (MKAO),

"Therefore, as God's chosen people, holy and dearly loved, clothe yourselves with compassion, kindness, humility, gentleness and patience. Bear with each other and forgive one another if any of you has a grievance against someone. Forgive as the Lord forgave you" (Col 3:12-13).

On Tuesday, August 8th, I was sitting at Grace in Growlers [a local restaurant], cruising with a few friends, new and old. Dylan, one of the young men there, checked his phone and saw that he had a text from his dad. Dylan was born and raised in Lahaina, and his entire family was still in Maui. His dad was texting about some fires.

On Wednesday, August 9th, Holly and Tim, leaders of Grace [one of our missional communities] and owners of Grace in Growlers, hear from Dylan, who happens to be one of their employees, that Lahaina has burned down overnight. Melissa, missional community leader of Our Kahuhipa, joins in with Tim and Holly and they work quickly to host an impromptu fundraiser event to give directly to Dylan's *ohana*'s [Hawaiian word meaning "family" or "kin"] needs. With MKAO's matching funds, direct giving, and total sales, Dylan's ohana received $8,000.

Tim received this message from Dylan's 'ohana:

Aloha,

My name is Liana, and I am part of the family of 9 (Ko 'Ohana). All of us lost everything, 2 vehicles, 2 houses, clothes, documents, cherished items that were passed down. Everything. We are all safe and have found us a temporary home. But with your help we were able to purchase to make our new place a home. We are so grateful for the love and support you have shown us, and I hope you know that you guys are the people the world needs more of.

Thank you again and we will always ALWAYS remember what you did for us!

Mahalo,

The Ko's

On Thursday and Friday, August 10 and 11, we did it again. After learning from MKAO's missional communities at large, two more families immediately affected by the wildfires contacted us. Haku, a missional community leader of Open Spaces told us of his *Tūtū's* [Hawaiian for "grandmother"] whole family, who for generations had been living in seven family properties that all burned down in Lahaina. Kex, a missional community leader of Na ʻOhana Leimana asked for assistance for his Aunty Noni and cousin Lani, whose home burned down in Lahaina. In quick partnership with representative leaders from both missional communities and Strong Support Teams, we pulled together generous donations to support these families with a gift of $7,500 each.

Kex's entire family, who are not Jesus followers, all came to support the fundraiser hosted at Grace in Growlers. Haku's coworkers from Kaʻōhao School came in support. Dylan brought his whole gang of friends in support; and that's when it happened. Dylan saw that MKAO had posted a picture of Kex's Aunty Noni and cousin Lani. He approached me and asked if I knew them personally, so I introduced him to Kex, who had never been to Grace in Growlers before. It turns out that Dylan is Lani's grandchild's godfather and that Lani's son and he are best friends. The two men wept together, understanding the depth of suffering they were bearing from being so far away from their loved ones in Lahaina.

On Tuesday, August 15, I got a phone call from Kex. Throughout the week, we heard stories about a man named Bini (Benny), who was like an angel during the fires in Lahaina, helping *kupuna*, including Aunty Noni, who is wheelchair bound and a dialysis patient, by carrying them over the sea rock wall, over the reef, and into safe waters. He kept them safe for over eight and a half hours, treading ocean water throughout the night until they were rescued by the Coast Guard. Kex called to tell me that his family had found Bini.

On Sunday, August 20, again through the quick and faithful work of MKAO's shared leadership, we hosted a fundraiser with all proceeds going to Bini, who has no family and also lost everything in the wildfires. We raised almost $7,000 to give directly to this hero. But the most significant thing happened that evening: at 6:00 p.m., we held a *Pule* (prayer) for Maui. Over one hundred people gathered in the taproom, 90 percent of whom were non–Jesus followers. I started off by sharing Bini's story and why we wanted to gather to raise a toast for this man. Then Kex contacted Bini for a video chat, so Bini participated in the *Pule* service. Then Kex's mom messaged Aunty Noni for a video chat, so her whole family joined the *Pule* service.

Roz, one of our missional community leaders from Na 'Ohana Leimana, opened with a prayer of welcome and an invitation for God's Spirit to come to this taproom. Meli, from our Vision Team, offered a poignant teaching on lament and the value God's people hold because we are a people of both lament and hope. Craig, another missional community leader from Na 'Ohana Leimana, invited us to commune with God through Colossians 3:12-14. And then Kex prayed a prayer of benediction for everyone in the room before we raised a glass for Bini. It was the first time Kex's family heard him pray.

On Tuesday, August 22, Kex received a message from Bini:

> The care and support from your family gives me instantaneous access to my best self and a feeling of overwhelming pure gratitude for the people in my life. There are at least a billion people on earth that would consider their prayers answered if they could trade places with me. To have my health, even just sort of. To have friends, even only a few; to have hobbies or interests or even the freedom to pursue them. To have spent this day free from some

terrifying encounter with chaos is to be lucky. Your family and friends' generosity is going to bring tranquility to my life as I begin to rebuild again. I truly can't thank you enough. No words can express my gratitude. Ultimately, progress is hard, but your blessing is as good an opportunity as I'm likely to have that can allow for some wisdom to emerge that considers the big picture and be of service and improve my life. Thank you all so very much.

These are just snippets from a long and detailed timeline that reveals once again just how much the kind of work and missional living we are doing in MKAO matters. The discipleship we have been equipped in to tether our lives to our neighbors has poised MKAO to be able to respond quickly, thoughtfully, and compassionately. It is in the times of chaos and crisis when character and a people's values aren't forged; they are revealed. MKAO's profound character of generosity, shared leadership, self-giving love, and value for being boundlessly present in the community around us is unmatched. Honored to do life with each of you,
Eun

In just two weeks' time, our pioneering church that values sharing leadership, stood soundly on our nimble collaborative ties, lived fully into our unique APEST leadership, and provided spaces where people experienced sending, liberating, welcoming, healing, and learning environments. We not only raised nearly $40,000 in that small window of time, but we drew the eyes and hearts and minds of an outside community who watched us treat them as we treat one another.

The same can be true of your church and community. May you go and do likewise.

AFTERWORD

DAVID E. FITCH

WHAT WILL BECOME of church leadership after Christendom?

This question spins in the minds of many of us living in post-Christendom cultures. Christendom describes a culture that aligns with Christianity, supports its beliefs, and upholds its structures and role in society. People are conditioned to look up to the pastor with unquestioned respect. Christian hierarchy can work in such a culture. But this Christendom culture is slipping away before our very eyes. As a result, hierarchical leadership has a short shelf life. We need a new path forward.

Eun Strawser's *You Were Never Meant to Lead Alone* offers such a path, out of hierarchical ways of leadership into the "fullness of Christ" (Eph 4:13), the fivefold ministry of the gifts of the Spirit "to equip his people" (Eph 4:12) for the ministry of the whole church. She offers a way to structure such leadership. She offers stories that give us courage to start in this direction. She offers a vision for the power that is unleashed in the practice of shared leadership. It could not have come at a more crucial time.

Eun's book seeks a return to the leadership model of the early church. The New Testament church, including the apostle Paul, exercised a leadership "among," a leadership "with," as opposed to a leadership "over" people. The early church took seriously Jesus' words, "You know that those who are supposed to rule over the Gentiles lord it over them. . . . But it shall not be so among you" (Mk 10:42-43 RSV). And this church flourished in mission under persecution without hierarchy.

Eun helps us understand what it might look like to return to such New Testament forms of leadership, to leave behind a leadership "over" people and return to the vibrant leadership of being "with" a people, "under" the power of the risen Christ at work "among" us.

I believe the church in the West is currently firmly located in the fields of mission. The church therefore must now be among people and the neighborhoods. It must engage, listen, collaborate, and discern the Spirit at work among us. The gifts of the Spirit must be cultivated and unleashed. Leadership that is top-down is not built for this. Shared leadership, mutually dependent on one another in the Spirit, is where we must start if we seek to cultivate churches into the mission of God at work in our neighborhoods.

For those of us now ministering in post-Christendom, who face challenges to authority from every corner, hierarchical leadership is exhausting. We are trying to herd cats, to keep things from falling apart. Hierarchical leadership no longer functions. Hierarchical leadership excludes marginalized people and women in ministry. We see homogenized churches that look the same as their leader. This is not the kingdom. We were not meant to lead like this, alone at the top. But we have no imagination for any other kind of leadership.

You Were Never Meant to Lead Alone offers us the imagination we need for this crucial moment. Eun gives us places to start this journey. Surely there will be many bumps in the road. There will be naysayers who maintain that this will never work. But Eun and her church are an example we can learn from in getting through what we must get through to go where we need to go.

I pray we receive this book as a gift for our times. And may the Lord bless all who pick up the cross of this kind of leadership for the challenging times we face leading Christ's church into mission.

ACKNOWLEDGMENTS

THE PHRASE "HAWAIKI RISING" is what the 'ohana wa'a, or family of Hawaiian voyaging canoes, say when they see land rising on the horizon. It's the nautical concept of raising land from the sea as when the voyagers on the Hokule'a raised Hawaii from the sea. It indeed takes an entire 'ohana to see a book rising on the horizon, and writing *You Were Never Meant to Lead Alone* felt like that from beginning to end. The story of sharing leadership is never stagnant; it waxes and wanes. And when you write about leadership and not leading alone, it inevitably becomes a personal story, and one that requires wading through my journey from aloneness to shared. I wept reliving some of the traumas of leadership abuse in writing this book, but I also shed tears of relief remembering the faithfulness of God in experiencing the gift of sharing leadership in real life.

To my Ma Ke Alo o 'ohana, I feel like I won the church leadership jackpot when I think of each of you. You are the gratitude linchpin in my being stretched large in leadership. Kelci and Paige, Melissa and Gabe, Roz and Craig, Laine, Mars, Haku, Keven, Timmy and Thaisa, Tim and Holly, Kex and Randi, Joel and Lela, Aunty Marlene, Aunty Jane, Uncle Bob, Aunty Liz and Aunty Irene, Haley, Bari, Linda, and Kathy, I honor each of you more than words can do justice. I could write volumes of books detailing each of the ways you exhibit mature sharing leadership. Ed and Mark, whenever people mistake my APEST as Shepherd gifting, I give you both all the credit! We have weathered so much of this church leadership journey together, and I honestly could not be the leader I am today without you. Meli and Hanzo, truly, I see the best of humanity in the two of you. If sharing leadership is the antidote to the poison of hierarchical church leadership, then every church needs a Meli and a Hanzo. Our partnership is my favorite one.

To my CCDA ʻohana, I cannot imagine leading in any ministry setting in this chaotic world without the grounding force each of you has been. Pastor Lorenzo, Christina, MaryBeth, and Scott; Bethany, Pastah J, Vatreisha, Joe, Mary, JR, Marie, Terrance, Darryl, Trishonda, Nilwona, Christian, Donna, Coach, Sandra, Kathy, Jerome, John, Dina, and Mayra, I am honestly in awe of you. Whenever I'm in those board meetings, I'm aghast that I'm a Christian because of the intensely faithful and hospitable lives you all live. Each of you has normalized the power of sharing leadership well before it will one day be status quo.

To my ʻIwa Collaborative ʻohana, what a gift it is to fly high and live low with each of you. Cory, Kyuboem, Ben, Amy, Matthew, Darryl, Sterling, Trishonda, Ricky, and Ray, I would subscribe to hierarchical church leadership if any one of you were at the top. But then again, you would each quickly turn it into shared leadership and give all your power away. Josh, if every leader got an opportunity to lead alongside you, the world would be devoid of abuse of power and this book would be instantly obsolete. You model humility, honor, hospitality, and hope better than anyone else I know.

To my editor, Al Hsu, thank you for your impeccable advice and far better arrangement of words and thoughts. To have a seasoned writer and author be at your editing helm is a treasure. To more foodie adventures and spicy Taiwanese food!

To my children, Beren, Emma, and Kyriella, you each test my humility because of how I burst with absolute pride in you three. You overshadow my ability to honor others because of how deeply you honor me. And you have inherited the prime gift of hospitality. You make me more hopeful in this world than sometimes I feel like I ought to be. I love you 3,000.

To my husband, Steve, thank you for bearing witness to my life. Even in my loneliest times of leadership, I was never *really* alone. You made space for all my wounds, never once dismissed them, and encouraged giving voice to them. I've discovered a deeper sense of joy because of how you held my grief with me. I've experienced a deeper sense of healing because of how you held my grief up to Jesus time and time again. I love you more than words can tell.

NOTES

PROLOGUE

1. THE NATURE OF LEADERSHIP

[1]Shara Drimalla and BibleProject Team, "What Are Sin, Iniquity, and Transgression in the Bible?," *Bible Project*, February 24, 2023, https://bibleproject.com/articles/sin-iniquity-and-transgression-in-the-bible/.

[2]Adam Dodds, *The Mission of the Triune God: Trinitarian Missiology in the Tradition of Lesslie Newbigin* (Eugene, OR: Pickwick, 2017), chap. 1, Kindle.

[3]Lorrin Andrews, *Dictionary of the Hawaiian Language*, s.v. "nei," (Honolulu: Henry M. Whitney, 1865), https://puke.ulukau.org/ulukau-books/?a=d&d=EBOOK-ANDREW.2.3.10.12&e=-------en-20--1--txt-txPT.

[4]Tim McKee, "The Geography of Sorrow: Francis Weller on Navigating Our Losses," *Sun Magazine*, October 2015, www.thesunmagazine.org/articles/27277-the-geography-of-sorrow.

[1]The Christian response to Warren Zevon's "I'll sleep when I'm dead" is often "I'll sleep when I'm in heaven."

[2]Paula Vidal Castelli, "The Burden of Leadership: Addressing Loneliness," *Forbes*, May 3, 2023, www.forbes.com/councils/forbescoachescouncil/2023/05/03/the-burden-of-leadership-addressing-loneliness/; and David Staal, "It's Lonely at the Top," *Christianity Today*, March 31, 2016, www.christianitytoday.com/2016/03/its-lonely-at-top-leadership/.

[3]Ken Walker, "Is Buying Your Way onto the Bestseller List Wrong?," *Christianity Today*, January/February 2015, www.christianitytoday.com/ct/2015/januaryfebruary/buying-bestsellers-resultsource.html; Bobby Ross Jr., "Sex, Money . . . Pride? Why Pastors Are Stepping Down," *Christianity Today*, July 14, 2011, www.christianitytoday.com/ct/2011/julyweb-only/sexmoneypride.html; and Kate Shellnutt, "Acts 29 CEO Removed Amid 'Accusations of Abusive Leadership,'" *Christianity Today*, February 7, 2020, www.christianitytoday.com/news/2020/february/acts-29-ceo-steve-timmis-removed-spiritual-abuse-tch.html.

[4]Warren Bennis, *On Becoming a Leader* (New York: Basic Books, 2009), chap. 1, Kindle.

[5]The Great Man Theory popularized in the 1840s by Thomas Carlyle states that leadership is intrinsic in some and exposed in appropriate situations. Thomas Carlyle, "On Heroes, Hero-Worship, and the Heroic in History," *Project Gutenberg*, [May 5, 1840] accessed January 2, 2025, www.gutenberg.org/files/1091/1091-h/1091-h.htm.

[6]Behavioral theory's contribution in the 1940s, which espoused the training of extrinsic skills in managerial leaders. Horace E. Johns and H. Ronald Moser, "From Trait to Transformation: The Evolution of Leadership Theories," *Education* 110 (1989): 115.

[7]Barna Group, "Christians on Leadership, Calling and Career," *Barna*, June 3, 2013, www.barna.com/research/christians-on-leadership-calling-and-career/.

[8]Keith R. Krispin Jr., "Christian Leader Development: An Outcomes Framework," *Christian Education Journal* 17, no. 1 (2019), https://journals.sagepub.com/doi/10.1177/0739891319869697.

[9]Isabel Wilkerson, *Caste: The Origins of Our Discontents* (New York: Random House, 2020), chap. 6, Kindle.

[10]Nijay K. Gupta, *Tell Her Story: How Women Led, Taught, and Ministered in the Early Church* (Downers Grove, IL: IVP Academic, 2023), 78.

[11]Gupta, *Tell Her Story*, 33.

[12]Alan Kreider, *The Patient Ferment of the Early Church: The Improbable Rise of Christianity in the Roman Empire* (Grand Rapids, MI: Baker Academic, 2016), chap. 4, Kindle.

[13]William Craig, "The Nature of Leadership in a Flat Organization," *Forbes*, October 23, 2018, updated April 14, 2022, www.forbes.com/sites/williamcraig/2018/10/23/the-nature-of-leadership-in-a-flat-organization/.

[14]Gupta, *Tell Her Story*, 80.

[15]Soong-Chang Rah, *The Next Evangelicalism: Freeing the Church from Western Cultural Captivity* (Downers Grove, IL: InterVarsity Press, 2009), 107.

[16]Gupta, *Tell Her Story*, 92-93.

[17]Sam Low, *Hawaiki Rising: Hōkūleʻa, Nainoa Thompson, and the Hawaiian Renaissance* (Honolulu: Island Heritage Publishing, 2013).

[18]"Ka Papa ʻŌlelo Hawaiʻi," *Hawaiian Language History & Revitalization*, www.kapapaolelohawaii.com/timeline.html.

[19]Jennifer Fahrni, "Princess Kaiulani: Her Life and Times," *The Kaʻiulani Project*, http://princesskaiulaniproject.com/about_princess_kaiulani.htm.

2. SHARING LEADERSHIP REQUIRES MATURITY

[1]Barna Group, "Christians on Leadership, Calling and Career," *Barna*, June 3, 2013, www.barna.com/research/christians-on-leadership-calling-and-career/.

[2]Barna Group, "3 Things Church Leaders Must Know as They Navigate Election Season," *Barna*, October 21, 2020, www.barna.com/research/lead-election-season/.

[3]Barna, "3 Things Church Leaders Must Know as They Navigate Election Season."

[4]Jade Scipioni, "These 2 Personality Traits Can Help Determine Whether You Get a Promotion or High Salary," *CNBC*, April 24, 2022, www.cnbc.com/2022/04/24/report-personality-traits-correlate-with-promotions-high-salaries.html.

[5]Katherine Schaeffer, "The Changing Face of Congress in 8 Charts," *Pew Research Center*, February 7, 2023, www.pewresearch.org/short-reads/2023/02/07/the-changing-face-of -congress/.

[6]Marius Marici, Remus Runcan, Iasmına Iosim, and Alexandra Haisan, "The Effect of Attire Attractiveness on Students' Perception of Their Teachers," *Secondary Educational Psychology* 13 (2022), www.frontiersin.org/journals/psychology/articles/10.3389/fpsyg .2022.1059631/full.

[7]Barna Group, "7-Year Trends: Pastors Feel More Loneliness & Less Support," *Barna*, July 12, 2023, www.barna.com/research/pastor-support-systems/; and Barna Group, "3 Things Church Leaders Must Know as They Navigate Election Season."

[8]Soong-Chan Rah, *The Next Evangelicalism: Freeing the Church from Western Cultural Captivity* (Downers Grove, IL: InterVarsity Press, 2009), 56.

[9]Jay Kim, "How to Church Shop Like the First Christians," *Christianity Today,* January 20, 2022, www.christianitytoday.com/ct/2022/january-web-only/covid-church-hopping -shopping-new-year-trend.html.

[10]I write extensively on this in E. K. Strawser, *Centering Discipleship: A Pathway for Multi- plying Spectators into Mature Disciples* (Downers Grove, IL: InterVarsity Press, 2023), 115.

[11]Dietrich Bonhoeffer, *Life Together: The Classic Exploration of Christian Community* (London: SCM Press, 1954), chap. 1, Kindle.

[12]I write more extensively on this in Strawser, *Centering Discipleship*, 123.

[13]Hermant Kakkar and Niro Sivanathan, "When the Appeal of a Dominant Leader Is Greater Than a Prestige Leader," *Psychological and Cognitive Sciences* 114, no. 26 (2017), www.pnas.org/doi/full/10.1073/pnas.1617711114.

3. MATURE LEADERS ARE DISCIPLES FIRST

[1]Robert C. Linthicum, *City of God, City of Satan: A Biblical Theology of the Urban Church* (Grand Rapids, MI: Zondervan, 1991), 292.

[2]Nils W. Lund, *Chiasmus in the New Testament: A Study in the Form and Function of Chiastic Structures* (1942; repr. Peabody, MA: Hendrickson, 1992), 40.

[3]Soong-Chan Rah, *The Next Evangelicalism: Freeing the Church from Western Cultural Captivity* (Downers Grove, IL: InterVarsity Press, 2009), 106-7.

[4]Rah, *Next Evangelicalism*, 107.

[5]David O. Moberg, *The Great Reversal: Reconciling Evangelism and Social Concern* (New York: J. B. Lippincott, 2007), 25-26.

[6]Christine D. Pohl, *Living into Community: Cultivating Practices That Sustain Us* (Grand Rapids, MI: Eerdmans, 2012), chap. 1, Kindle.

[7]I write extensively on this in E. K. Strawser, *Centering Discipleship: A Pathway for Multi- plying Spectators into Mature Disciples* (Downers Grove, IL: InterVarsity Press, 2023), 36-38.

[8]Dietrich Bonhoeffer, *The Cost of Discipleship* (New York: Touchstone, 1995), 59.

[9]Henri J. M. Nouwen, *The Selfless Way of Christ: Downward Mobility and the Spiritual Life* (Maryknoll, NY: Orbis Books, 2007), Kindle, chap. 3.

[10]Nouwen, *Selfless Way of Christ*, chap. 3.

[11]M. Craig Barnes, *The Pastor as Minor Poet: Texts and Subtexts in the Ministerial Life* (Grand Rapids, MI: Eerdmans, 2008), 49.

[12]Rachel Treisman, "Maui's Wildfires Are Among the Deadliest on Record in the U.S. Here Are Some Others," *NPR*, August 15, 2023, www.npr.org/2023/08/15/1193710165 /maui-wildfires-deadliest-us-history.

4. THE 4 Hs: MARKS OF MATURE LEADERS

[1]Hasan Minhaj, *Off with His Head*, Netflix, 2024.

[2]Nijay K. Gupta, *Tell Her Story: How Women Led, Taught, and Ministered in the Early Church* (Downers Grove, IL: IVP Academic, 2023), chap. 5, Kindle.

[3]Gupta, *Tell Her Story*, chap. 5.

[4]Hebrews 12:2 links maturity to self-giving love in the example of Christ. The author of Hebrews is saying that as we focus on Jesus, the one who matures us (*teleiōtēs*), let us pay attention to how he does this. He matures us through self-giving (*kenōsis*) love on the cross, not paying mind to its shame. Why? Because he never lost sight of where he was headed (*telos*).

[5]Dawn Reiss, "Why Maya Angelou Disliked Modesty," *Atlantic*, June 2, 2014, www .theatlantic.com/entertainment/archive/2014/06/why-maya-angelou-didnt-believe-in -modesty/371965/.

[6]*Blue Letter Bible*, s.v. *harpagmos*, Strong's G725, www.blueletterbible.org/lexicon/g725 /kjv/tr/0-1/.

[7]Karin S. Frey, Adaurennaya C. Onyewuenyi, Shelley Hymel, Randip Gill, and Cynthia R Pearson, "Honor, Face, and Dignity Norm Endorsement Among Diverse North American Adolescents: Development of a Social Norms Survey," *International Journal of Behavioral Development* 45, no. 3 (2020), https://doi.org/10.1177/0165025420949690; and Zeba Crook, "Honor, Shame and Social Status Revisited," *Journal of Biblical Literature* 128, no. 3 (2009): 591-611, https://doi.org/10.2307/25610205.

[8]Marilynne Robinson, *Gilead: A Novel* (New York: Farrar, Straus and Giroux, 2004), 139.

[9]J. K. Campbell, "Honor and the Devil," in *Honour and Shame: The Values of Mediterranean Society*, ed. J. G. Peristiany (London: Weidenfeld & Nicolson, 1966), 152.

[10]*Blue Letter Bible*, s.v. *kābôd*, Strong's H3519, www.blueletterbible.org/lexicon/h3519/kjv /wlc/0-1/.

[11]*Blue Letter Bible*, s.v. *kābad*, Strong's H3513, www.blueletterbible.org/lexicon/h3513/kjv /wlc/0-1/.

[12]Benedict Atkins, personal correspondence with author, September 27, 2021.

[13]Andrew T. Draper, Jody Michele, and Andrea Mae, *Disabling Leadership: A Practical Theology for the Broken Body of Christ* (Downers Grove, IL: IVP Academic, 2023), 4.

[14]Christine D. Pohl, *Living into Community: Cultivating Practices That Sustain Us* (Grand Rapids, MI: Eerdmans, 2012), chap. 4, Kindle.

[15]EHL Insights, "What Is the Hospitality Industry? All Your Questions Answered," EHL Insights, March 28, 2024, https://hospitalityinsights.ehl.edu/hospitality-industry; Julian Yudelson, "Adapting McCarthy's Four P's for the Twenty-First Century," *Journal of Marketing Education* 21, no. 1 (1999): 60-67.

[16]Anders Johansson, "Revamping the 4Ps: A Modern Guide for Hotel Marketing Success," *Demand Calendar*, August 1, 2023, www.demandcalendar.com/blog/revamping-the-4ps -a-modern-guide-for-hotel-marketing-success.

[17]Pohl, *Living into Community*, chap. 11.

[18]Alexia Salvatierra and Brandon Wrencher, *Buried Seeds: Learning from the Vibrant Resilience of Marginalized Christian Communities* (Grand Rapids, MI: Baker Academic, 2022), 84.

[19]Ibram X. Kendi, *How to Be an Antiracist* (New York: One World, 2019), chap. 4, Kindle.

[20]Crystal L. Hoyt, Lauren Aguilar, Cheryl R. Kaiser, Jim Blascovich, and Kevin Lee, "The Self-Protective and Undermining Effects of Attributional Ambiguity," *Journal of Experimental Social Psychology* 43, no. 6 (2007): 884-93.

[21]Salvatierra and Wrencher, *Buried Seeds*, 222-23, italics original.

[22]Isabel Wilkerson, *Caste: The Origins of Our Discontents* (New York: Random House, 2020), 357-58.

[23]Jennifer Teramoto Pedrotti, Lisa M. Edwards, and Shane J. Lopez, "Promoting Hope: Suggestions for School Counselors," *Professional School Counseling* 12, no. 2 (2008): 83, https://epublications.marquette.edu/cgi/viewcontent.cgi?article=1082&context =edu_fac.

[24]Lilly Shanahan, Sherika N. Hill, Lauren M. Gaydosh, Annekatrin Steinhoff, E. Jane Costello, Kenneth A. Dodge, Kathleen Mullan Harris, and Willam E. Copeland, "Does Despair Really Kill?: A Roadmap for an Evidence-Based Answer," *American Journal of Public Health* 109, no. 6 (2019): 855, https://ajph.aphapublications.org/doi/full/10.2105 /AJPH.2019.305016.

[25]Matthew Desmond and Adam Travis, "Political Consequences of Survival Strategies Among the Urban Poor," *American Sociological Review* 83, no. 5 (2018): 869.

[26]Shanahan et al., "Does Despair Really Kill?," 854-58

5. REVISING THE DELINEATION OF LEADERSHIP FROM EPHESIANS 4

[1]Alan Hirsch first popularized APEST through his book *The Forgotten Ways: Reactivating the Missional Church* (Grand Rapids, MI: Brazos Press, 2009); other key contributors are Tim Catchim with Alan Hirsch, *The Permanent Revolution: Apostolic Imagination and Practice for the 21st Century Church* (San Francisco: Jossey-Bass, 2012); and Neil Cole, *Primal Fire: Reigniting the Church with the Five Gifts of Jesus* (Carol Stream, IL: Tyndale Momentum, 2014).

[2]Alan Hirsch, *5Q: Reactivating the Original Intelligence and Capacity of the Body of Christ* (n.p.: 100 Movements, 2017).

[3]Michael Frost and Alan Hirsch, *The Shaping of Things to Come: Innovation and Mission for the 21st-Century Church* (Peabody, MA: Hendrickson, 2003), chap. 1, Kindle.

[4]Darryl Dash, "APEST: A Good Idea Taken Too Far," *The Gospel Coalition*, November 17, 2021, https://ca.thegospelcoalition.org/columns/straight-paths/apest-a-good-idea -taken-too-far/.

[5]Julia Mebane, *The Body Politic in Roman Political Thought* (Cambridge, UK: Cambridge University Press, 2024), 1.

[6]The Greek can be translated "pastors" or "shepherds," but for the purpose of delineation, I use the latter. See *Blue Letter Bible*, s.v. *poimēn*, Strong's G4166, www.blueletterbible .org/lexicon/g4166/kjv/tr/0-1/.

[7]Christine D. Pohl, *Living into Community: Cultivating Practices That Sustain Us* (Grand Rapids, MI: Eerdmans, 2012), chap. 1, Kindle.

[8]Cole, *Primal Fire*, 12.

6. REFRAMING APOSTLE, PROPHET, EVANGELIST, SHEPHERD, AND TEACHER LEADERS

[1]Jiaqi Xiong, Orly Lipsitz, Flora Nasri, Leanna M. W. Lui, Hartej Gill, Lee Phan, David Chen-Li, Michelle Iacobucci, Roger Ho, Amna Majeed, and Roger S. McIntyre, "Impact of COVID-19 Pandemic on Mental Health in the General Population: A Systematic Review," *Journal of Affective Disorders* 277 (2020): 55-64, https://doi.org/10.1016/j .jad.2020.08.001; and Mustafa Demir and Suyeon Park, "The Effect of COVID-19 on Domestic Violence and Assaults," *Criminal Justice Review* 47, no. 4 (2022): 445-63, https:// doi.org/10.1177/07340168211061160.

[2]Amy Roberson Hayes and Diamond Lee, "Women, Work, and Families During the COVID-19 Pandemic: Examining the Effects of COVID Policies and Looking to the Future," *Journal of Social Issues* 79, no. 3 (2022): 1088-1105, https://doi.org/10.1111/josi.12510.

[3]Tyra Jean, "Black Lives Matter: Police Brutality in the Era of COVID-19," *Lerner Center for Public Health Promotion and Population Health*, Syracuse University, June 2020, www .maxwell.syr.edu/research/lerner-center/population-health-research-brief-series /article/black-lives-matter-police-brutality-in-the-era-of-covid-19; Dror Walter, Yotam Ophir, and Hui Ye, "Conspiracies, Misinformation and Resistance to Public Health Mea- sures During COVID-19 in White Nationalist Online Communication," *Vaccine* 41, no. 17 (2023): 2868-77, https://doi.org/10.1016/j.vaccine.2023.03.050; and Angela R. Gover, Shannon B. Harper, and Lynn Langton, "Anti-Asian Hate Crime During the COVID-19 Pandemic: Exploring the Reproduction of Inequality," *American Journal of Criminal Justice* 45, no. 4 (2020): 647-67, https://link.springer.com/article/10.1007/s12103-020-09545-1.

[4]Michael Dimock and Richard Wike, "America Is Exceptional in the Nature of Its Po- litical Divide," *Pew Research Center*, November 13, 2020, www.pewresearch.org/short -reads/2020/11/13/america-is-exceptional-in-the-nature-of-its-political-divide/.

[5]Zenitha Prince, "Eleven O'Clock on Sundays Is Still the Most Segregated Hour in America," *Louisiana Weekly*, June 15, 2016, www.louisianaweekly.com/eleven-oclock-on -sundays-is-still-the-most-segregated-hour-in-america/.

[6]Barna Group, "3 Things Church Leaders Must Know as They Navigate Election Season," *Barna*, October 21, 2020, www.barna.com/research/lead-election-season/.

[7]E. K. Strawser, *Centering Discipleship: A Pathway for Multiplying Spectators into Mature Disciples* (Downers Grove, IL: InterVarsity Press, 2023), chap. 7, Kindle.

[8]Soong-Chan Rah, *Prophetic Lament: A Call for Justice in Troubled Times* (Downers Grove, IL: InterVarsity Press, 2015), 182.

[9]*Oxford Learner's Dictionary*, s.v. "equip," accessed January 3, 2025, www.oxfordlearners dictionaries.com/us/definition/english/equip.

[10]*Blue Letter Bible*, s.v. *katartismós*, Strong's G2677, www.blueletterbible.org/lexicon /g2677/kjv/tr/0-1/.

[11]*Merriam-Webster Dictionary*, s.v. "render," accessed January 3, 2025, www.merriam -webster.com/dictionary/render.

7. RELYING ON APEST FOR SHARING LEADERSHIP

[1]Alan Hirsch, *The Forgotten Ways: Reactivating the Missional Church* (Grand Rapids, MI: Brazos Press, 2009).

[2]Lesslie Newbigin, *The Gospel in a Pluralist Society* (Grand Rapids, MI: Eerdmans, 1989), chap. 19, Kindle.

[3]Hirsch, *Forgotten Ways*, 172.

8. RECALLING APEST FOR ALL TYPES OF SHARING LEADERS

[1]Scott Barkley, "Southern Baptists Pass First Approval of Constitutional Amendment over Women Pastors," *Baptist Press*, June 14, 2023, www.baptistpress.com/resource -library/news/southern-baptists-pass-first-approval-of-constitutional-amendment -over-women-pastors/.

[2]I write more extensively on this in Eun Strawser, "Loneliness Is the Penalty for Women Leaders," *Missio Alliance*, September 7, 2023, www.missioalliance.org/loneliness-is -the-penalty-for-women-leaders/.

[3]Ryan P. Burge, "Researcher: Most Evangelicals Support Women in Church Leadership," *Christianity Today*, June 30, 2020, www.christianitytoday.com/ct/2020/june-web-only /research-evangelicals-women-leaders-complementarian-preach.html.

[4]Frances C. Kneupper, "The Southern Baptist Convention's Case Against Female Pastors Is Centuries Old," *Washington Post*, June 22, 2023, www.washingtonpost.com/made-by -history/2023/06/22/southern-baptist-convention-female-pastors/.

[5]Carmen Joy Imes, "Being God's Image as a Woman in the Academy and the Church" *InterVarsity Press*, March 20, 2023, www.ivpress.com/pages/content/being-gods-image -woman-in-the-academy-and-the-church.

[6]Iris Marion Young, *Justice and the Politics of Difference*, rev. ed. (Princeton, NJ: Princeton University Press, 2011), chap. 1, Kindle.

[7]Leroy Barber with Velma Maia Thomas, *Red, Brown, Yellow, Black, White—Who's More Precious in God's Sight?: A Call for Diversity in Christian Missions and Ministry* (Nashville: Jericho Books, 2014), 5.

[8]Alexia Salvatierra and Brandon Wrencher, *Buried Seeds: Learning from the Vibrant Resilience of Marginalized Christian Communities* (Grand Rapids, MI: Baker Academic, 2022), 95.

[9]For this distinction, see Joshua Rothman, "The Meaning of 'Culture,'" *New Yorker*, December 26, 2014, www.newyorker.com/books/joshua-rothman/meaning-culture.

[10]See Cecilia Heyes, "Culture," *Current Biology* 30, no. 20 (2020): R1246-R1250, doi.org /10.1016/j.cub.2020.08.086.

[11]H. Richard Niebuhr, *Christ and Culture* (New York: Harper & Row, 1975), 32-33.

[12]Peter Bevington Smith and Michael Harris Bond, "Cultures and Persons: Characterizing National and Other Types of Cultural Differences Can Also Aid Our Understanding and Prediction of Individual Variability," *Frontiers in Psychology* 10 (2019): 2689, doi.10.3389/fpsyg.2019.02689.

[13]Robert Chao Romero, "The Immigrant Church and the Future of Christianity in the United States," *Robert Chao Romero* (blog), January 3, 2022, www.robertchaoromero .com/new-blog/2022/1/3/the-future-of-us-christianity-in-2050.

[14]Soojin Chung, "History of Korean Immigration to America, from 1903 to Present," *Boston Korean Diaspora Project*, Boston University School of Theology, https://sites .bu.edu/koreandiaspora/issues/history-of-korean-immigration-to-america-from-1903 -to-present/.

[15]Shruti Mukkamala and Karen L. Suyemoto, "From Exotic to Invisible: Asian American Women's Experiences of Discrimination," *American Psychological Association*, July 26, 2018, www.apa.org/pubs/highlights/spotlight/issue-119.

[16]Eun Strawser, "Assimilation Displaces, and the Church Is Complicit," *Missio Alliance*, May 28, 2024, www.missioalliance.org/assimilation-displaces-and-the-church-is -complicit/.

[17]Kate Coleman, *7 Deadly Sins of Women in Leadership: Overcome Self-Defeating Behavior in Work and Ministry*, updated ed. (Grand Rapids, MI: Zondervan, 2021), 166.

[18]Salvatierra and Wrencher, *Buried Seeds*, 28.

[19]Richard J. Mouw, *When the Kings Come Marching In: Isaiah and the New Jerusalem*, rev. ed. (Grand Rapids, MI: Eerdmans, 2002), chap. 4, Kindle.

[20]James Wright, "The White Gaze: Epistemological Imposition and Paradoxical Logic in Educational Research," *International Journal of Qualitative Studies in Education*, August 2023, 1-14, www.tandfonline.com/doi/full/10.1080/09518398.2023.2248051#.

[21]Jonathan Tran, *Asian Americans and the Spirit of Racial Capitalism* (Oxford, UK: Oxford University Press, 2021), 14, Kindle.

9. THE POWER OF SHARING LEADERSHIP

[1]In a personal conversation with Neil Cole, he taught me to set an alarm for 10:02 a.m. every day so that we can carve out space to do exactly this, and pray.

[2]Barna Group, "7-Year Trends: Pastors Feel More Loneliness & Less Support," *Barna*, July 12, 2023, www.barna.com/research/pastor-support-systems/.

[3]David E. Fitch, *Reckoning with Power: Why the Church Fails When It's on the Wrong Side of Power* (Grand Rapids, MI: Brazos Press, 2024), chap. 1, Kindle.

[4]Fitch, *Reckoning with Power*, chap. 1.

[5]Andrej Zaslove, Bram Geurkink, Kristof Jacobs, and Agnes Akkerman, "Power to the People?: Populism, Democracy, and Political Participation; A Citizen's Perspective," *West European Politics* 44 (2020): 727-51, doi:10.1080/01402382.2020.1776490.

[6]Iris Marion Young, *Justice and the Politics of Difference*, rev. ed. (Princeton, NJ: Princeton University Press, 2011), chap. 1, Kindle.

[7]Kristopher Norris, "The Problem Was Always Bigger Than Mark Driscoll," *Sojourners*, August 31, 2021, https://sojo.net/articles/problem-was-always-bigger-mark-driscoll.

[8]Sam Hailes, "Francis Chan: Why I Quit My Megachurch and Started Again," *Premier Christianity*, January 20, 2019, www.premierchristianity.com/interviews/francis-chan -why-i-quit-my-megachurch-and-started-again/1183.article.

[9]N. T. Wright, *The Day the Revolution Began: Reconsidering the Meaning of Jesus's Crucifixion* (New York: Harper One, 2016), 222.

[10]Young, *Justice and the Politics of Difference*, chap. 1, Kindle.

[11]Joseph W. Handley Jr., "Polycentric Mission Leadership: Toward a New Theoretical Model: OCMS Montagu Barker Lecture Series: 'Polycentric Theology, Mission, and Mission Leadership,'" *Transformation* 38, no. 3 (2021): 225-39, www.jstor.org/stable /27081866.

[12]Kirk J. Franklin, "A Paradigm for Global Mission Leadership: The Journey of the Wycliffe Global Alliance" (PhD thesis, University of Pretoria, 2016), http://hdl.handle .net/2263/53075.

[13]Nora Hamzeh, "Female Leaders and Distributed Leadership: What Can Women Bring to the Table?," *Open Journal of Leadership* 12, no. 1 (2023): 15-28, https://doi.org/10.4236 /ojl.2023.121002.

[14]Meredith Somers, "Why Distributed Leadership Is the Future of Management," *Ideas Made to Matter*, MIT Sloan School of Management, April 19, 2022, https://mitsloan.mit .edu/ideas-made-to-matter/why-distributed-leadership-future-management.

[15]I write extensively on this in in Eun Strawser, "Loneliness Is the Penalty for Women Leaders," *Missio Alliance*, September 7, 2023, www.missioalliance.org/loneliness-is-the -penalty-for-women-leaders/.

[16]The term *lazy* being applied to local, Indigenous people has been detrimental to the spiritual well-being of a people group already struggling with a Christian and Hawaiian

identity. There is more to be said on leaders learning first a culture of requesting permission before assuming lack of interest.

[17] Hae-Ra Han, Ashley Xu, Kyra J. W. Mendez, Safiyyah Okoye, Joycelyn Cudjoe, Mona Bahouth, Melanie Reese, Lee Bone, and Cheryl Dennison-Himmelfarb, "Exploring Community Engaged Research Experiences and Preferences: A Multi-level Qualitative Investigation," *Research Involvement and Engagement* 7, no. 19 (2021), https://doi.org/10.1186/s40900-021-00261-6.

[18] Borrowed from Pastor Cory Doiron, personal conversation with author, 2019.

10. HOW TO START SHARING LEADERSHIP

[1] Christine D. Pohl, *Living into Community: Cultivating Practices That Sustain Us* (Grand Rapids, MI: Eerdmans, 2012), chap. 1, Kindle.

[2] I write extensively on this in E. K. Strawser, *Centering Discipleship: A Pathway for Multiplying Spectators into Mature Disciples* (Downers Grove, IL: InterVarsity Press, 2023), 73, Kindle.

[3] *Hidden Figures*, directed by Theodore Melfi (20th Century Fox, 2016).

[4] N. T. Wright, *The Day the Revolution Began: Reconsidering the Meaning of Jesus's Crucifixion* (New York: Harper One, 2016), 278.

[5] *Blue Letter Bible*, s.v. *megas*, Strong's G3173, www.blueletterbible.org/lexicon/g3173/kjv/tr/0-1/.

[6] Note Jewish Levites beginning their priestly service at age thirty: Numbers 4:3, 23, 30, 35.

[7] Jennifer Manuel, "Practicing Kilo" (blog), *Mid-Pacific*, October 16, 2023, www.midpac.edu/academics/elementary-school/blogs/blogdetails/~board/principals-blog/post/20231016-elementaryblog-manuel.

11. HOW TO STRUCTURE SHARING LEADERSHIP

[1] Oliver Brooks, "Police Brutality and Blacks: An American Immune System Disorder," *Journal of the National Medical Association* 112, no. 3 (2020): 239-41, https://doi.org/10.1016/j.jnma.2020.06.003.

[2] Soong-Chan Rah, *The Next Evangelicalism: Freeing the Church from Western Cultural Captivity* (Downers Grove, IL: InterVarsity Press, 2009), 29-30.

[3] David Roach, "In Church Planting, More Money Means More People," *Christianity Today*, January 3, 2023, www.christianitytoday.com/ct/2023/januaryfebruary/church-planting-costs-startup-money-metrics.html.

[4] Kevin D. Dougherty, Mark Chaves, and Michael O. Emerson, "Racial Diversity in U.S. Congregations, 1998–2019," *Journal for the Scientific Study of Religion* 59, no. 4 (2020): 651-62, https://doi.org/10.1111/jssr.12681.

[5] Gerardo Martí, *American Blindspot: Race, Class, Religion and the Trump Presidency* (Lanham, MD: Rowman & Littlefield, 2020), introduction, Kindle.

⁶Korie L. Edwards, *The Elusive Dream: The Power of Race in Interracial Churches* (Oxford, UK: Oxford University Press, 2008), chap. 1, Kindle.

⁷Yonat Shimron, "Study: Multiracial Churches Are Growing, but Racial Unity May Be Elusive," *Washington Post*, November 13, 2020, www.washingtonpost.com/religion /study-multiracial-churches-are-growing-but-racial-unity-may-be-elusive/2020/11/13 /d688163a-25b6-11eb-8672-c281c7a2c96e_story.html.

⁸Sheryl Sandberg, *Lean In: Women, Work, and the Will to Lead* (New York: Knopf, 2013), chap. 5, Kindle.

⁹Sylvia Ann Hewlett, with Kerrie Peraino, Laura Sherbin, and Karen Sumberg, "The Sponsor Effect: Breaking Through the Last Glass Ceiling," *Harvard Business Review*, January 12, 2011, https://wearethecity.com/wp-content/uploads/2014/10/The-Sponsor -Effect.pdf.

¹⁰Sandberg, *Lean In*, chap. 5.

¹¹My community is currently working on renaming our community and those we have fostered given the undertones of colonization from the word *missional*, particularly in an area where White evangelical colonization of the Hawaiian culture has taken place in recent history.

¹²*Erin Brockovich*, directed by Steven Soderbergh (Universal Pictures, 2000).

12. HOW TO SUSTAIN SHARING LEADERSHIP

¹Soong-Chan Rah, *The Next Evangelicalism: Freeing the Church from Western Cultural Captivity* (Downers Grove, IL: InterVarsity Press, 2009), 56.

²Kyuboem Lee, "What Will Keep Us from Building a Church in the Ruins?," *Missio Alliance*, October 13, 2021, www.missioalliance.org/what-will-keep-us-from-building -a-church-in-the-ruins/.

³Jonathan Brooks, *Church Forsaken: Practicing Presence in Neglected Neighborhoods* (Downers Grove, IL: InterVarsity Press, 2018), 15.

⁴Christine D. Pohl, *Living into Community: Cultivating Practices That Sustain Us* (Grand Rapids, MI: Eerdmans, 2012), chap. 1, Kindle.

⁵Alan Kreider, *The Patient Ferment of the Early Church: The Improbable Rise of Christianity in the Roman Empire* (Grand Rapids, MI: Baker Academic, 2016), chap. 6, Kindle.

⁶Lesslie Newbigin, *The Open Secret: An Introduction to the Theology of Mission* (Grand Rapids, MI: Eerdmans, 1978), 127.

⁷Dietrich Bonhoeffer, *The Cost of Discipleship* (New York: Touchstone, 1995), 59.

⁸"About," *Christian Community Development Association*, emphasis original, https:// ccda.org/about/.

⁹Jonathan Tran, *Asian Americans and the Spirit of Racial Capitalism* (Oxford, UK: Oxford University Press, 2021), 219.

¹⁰Fox 32 Digital Staff, "These Are Chicago's 10 Most Dangerous Neighborhoods, According to PropertyClub," *Fox 32 Chicago*, January 3, 2024, www.fox32chicago.com /news/chicago-most-dangerous-neighborhoods; and Jackson Morsey, Alex Linares,

Jack Rocha, and Matthew D. Wilson, "Lawndale Service Area Databook," *Great Cities Institute*, August 2021, https://greatcities.uic.edu/wp-content/uploads/2022/04/NorthLawndaleDatabookSmall.pdf.

[11]"Our History," *The Lawndale Miracle*, Lawndale Christian Health Center, accessed January 4, 2025, https://lawndale.org/our-history.

EPILOGUE

[1]Richard Rohr, *Falling Upward: A Spirituality for the Two Halves of Life* (Hoboken, NJ: Jossey-Bass, 2011), 101.

ABOUT THE AUTHOR

REV. DR. EUN K. STRAWSER IS the co-vocational co-lead pastor of Ma Ke Alo o (which means "presence" in Hawaiian) missional communities multiplying in Honolulu, Hawaii; a community physician; contributing writer for Missio Alliance; and adjunct professor at the Leland Center for Theological Studies and Northern Seminary. She is also the author of *Centering Discipleship: A Pathway for Multiplying Spectators into Mature Disciples* (Downers Grove, IL: InterVarsity Press, 2023), contributing author to *The Starter's Way: Leading New Contextual Christian Communities* (New York: Church Publishing, forthcoming), and the cofounder of 'Iwa Collaborative, a consulting and content-developing firm created to equip kingdom-grounded leaders to center discipleship and remission church in their local place. She also serves on the executive board for the Christian Community Development Association (CCDA). Prior to transitioning to Hawaii, she served as adjunct professor of medicine at the Philadelphia College of Medicine and of African Studies at her alma mater, the University of Pennsylvania (where she and her husband served with InterVarsity Christian Fellowship) after finishing her Fulbright Scholarship at the University of Dar es Salaam. She and Steve have three seriously amazing children.

www.ekstrawser.com
Instagram @ekstrawser

'Iwa Collaborative
eun@iwacollaborative.com
www.iwacollaborative.com
Instagram @iwacollaborative

Ma Ke Alo o (MKAO),
Co-lead pastor
eun@mkao.community
www.mkao.community
Instagram @mkao.community

ALSO BY THE AUTHOR

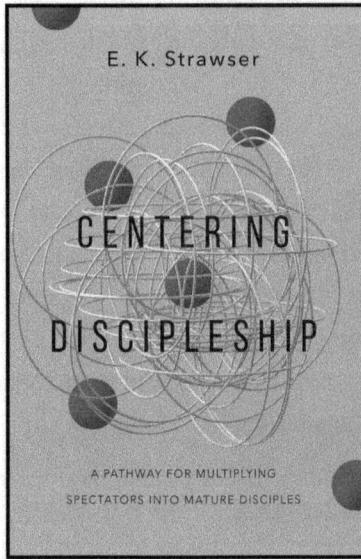

Centering Discipleship
978-1-5140-0706-8

Missio Alliance

Rooted in the core convictions of evangelical orthodoxy, the ministry of Missio Alliance is animated by a strong and distinctive theological identity that emphasizes comprehensive mutuality, hopeful witness, and the church in mission. Missio Alliance addresses the most vital theological and cultural issues facing the North American church in God's mission today. In partnership with InterVarsity Press, Missio Alliance offers a line of books authored by a diverse range of theological practitioners. These resources are selected based on how they address and embody these values and the unique contribution they offer in equipping Christian leaders for fuller and more faithful participation in God's mission.

Remissioning Church
978-1-5140-1055-6

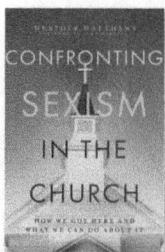

Confronting Sexism in the Church
978-1-5140-0818-8

Faithful Politics
978-1-5140-0749-5

Plundered
978-1-5140-0774-7

Centering Discipleship
978-1-5140-0706-8

Finding Freedom in Constraint
978-1-5140-0431-9

missioalliance.org | ✗ ⓕ ⓘ | missioalliance

C|C   CHRISTIAN COMMUNITY
D|A   DEVELOPMENT ASSOCIATION

The Christian Community Development Association (CCDA) is a network of Christians committed to engaging with people and communities in the process of transformation. For over thirty-five years, CCDA has aimed to inspire, train, and connect Christians who seek to bear witness to the kingdom of God by reclaiming and restoring under-resourced communities. CCDA walks alongside local practitioners and partners as they live out Christian Community Development (CCD) by loving their neighbors.

Front Porch Wisdom
978-1-5140-0888-1

Worth Seeing
978-1-5140-0712-9

Persevering Power
978-1-5140-0847-8

Join the Resistance
978-1-5140-0433-3

Brown Church
978-0-8308-5285-7

Church Forsaken
978-0-8308-4555-2